BORDERLINE ODDITIES

FOR THE MILLIONS

"For the Millions" Series

BORDERLINE ODDITIES
FOR THE MILLIONS

edited by Shelly Lowenkopf

FOR THE MILLIONS SERIES

SHERBOURNE PRESS, INC.   LOS ANGELES, CALIFORNIA

CONTENTS

5

INTRODUCTION

Among the millions of potential and real experiences in store for the vast majority of people on earth, there is a significant type, simultaneously one of the most common and one of the most disputed. This unique category is the Borderline experience, and it is quite probable to assume that individuals both primitive and civilized have been involved in it since the beginning of time—and arguing about its significance just as long.

The Borderline experience may be the result of a crude fetish made by a New Guinea native or the result of the medicine dream of an American Plains Indian. But it may also mean a motion picture contract to a Hollywood starlet who follows astrology or a communion with God by a college student who is high on LSD.

Borderline experiences take place in waking or sleeping states, day or night, indoors or outside. In them, persons allegedly have communications with beings long dead or beings in other worlds. But they also have non-mechanical communications with living persons in the next room or the next city.

This is a world where hunches come true, warnings of impending peril are given, long lost articles are recovered, and individuals suddenly find themselves in the possession of information which was not available to them through readily demonstrable channels.

Countless words and expressions have been coined to help explain these various phenomena and the words cause nearly as much trouble as the occurrences themselves. There are several types of ghosts which are named according to gender, intent, and appearance, if any. Still, with all this classification, we do not know positively that a poltergeist cannot perform some of the same activities of an incubus or, indeed, if the same being that is an incubus might not also be a poltergeist.

Some scientific-sounding terms have crept into the supernatural lexicon over the centuries, yet it is quite possible for arguments to arise over the comparative shadings of telekinesis, psychokinesis, and teleportation. Paranormal, supernormal, supernatural, and psychic phenomena are ways of saying the same thing: we don't know *what* happened, but we think something highly unusual took place.

Among the critics and devotees of psychic phenomena are those who insist that the expression "mental telepathy" is redundant; telepathy is enough by itself. Still others believe the entire concept of ESP is nonsense since it cannot be repeated at will the way, for example, water may be brought to a boil at the same temperature.

Often, the world of reality is invaded by an invention or system from the Borderline world; a perfectly ingenious invention or a completely logical system for which there is no known use or application. Such a system was *analysis situs*, more popularly known as topology. An almost completely independent branch of geometry, topology

8

treated with consistent logic certain spatial properties of materials. A strip of paper, for instance, could be folded in such a way as to leave it with only one side. So what? This one-sided strip, called a moibus strip, was also found to be a cross section of a Klein bottle, a container which was significant for having its mouth in its bottom and its bottom in its mouth. Again, so what? And why should grown men concern themselves with finding something to put in a Klein bottle, anyway? In a matter of a few years, however, topology was found to have uses, and our technology has developed enough to include it, relate it, and use it with profit. But there is still the matter of silly putty, which is still functional only as a toy, remarkable physical properties notwithstanding.

There is undoubtedly a link between the Borderline world and the world of scientific fact, but believers in the world of Borderline phenomena claim science is too stodgy and limiting (a matter which will be discussed in this book at length by Joseph F. Goodavage), while most scientists will shrug off the Borderline as irrational and undisciplined at best. Yet both camps freely admit there is an abundance of human and physical behavior for which we have no explanation and for which we look to the future for more information.

Individuals are jealous of their Borderline experiences. Unlike the manner in which they discuss the most intimate details of their lives at the slightest invitation, they often require strong assurances of respect and belief in their sanity before divulging one encounter with the supernatural. Once the cork is out, however, there may be an embarrassment of riches. Dreams, spirits, sightings, and strange talents will come oozing forth . . . along with

9

future protestations that the whole conversation was only in jest.

Famous persons in the arts, sciences, and literature are quite willing to stake their reputations on one painting, one book, or one discovery from their creative process, yet they are covert in their public reactions to the world of ESP. On the other hand, they don't seem to care if their love lives or political affiliations, no matter how radical or conservative, are broadcast widely.

This book is merely a hinting at the dimensions of the Borderline world. Prophesies, inventions, mysterious cures, and strange events are only a part of it. There is also the little matter of pressures.

Past events have taught us never to expect a liberal climate from the Borderline world, only devotees and detractors. More often than not, the devotees are placed in a position of looking on with sympathy and helplessness while the detractors hold forth against too outspoken a stand for the Borderline world.

There is no comfort in assuming the inquisitions, witch hunts, and suppressions are all a part of history. Less than fifty years ago, a member of the medical profession was imprisoned and certain of his works burned. The man was Wilhelm Reich who, even today, is a public anathema but a private source of riches to many doctors.

And just to round out the picture, the trustee of the Wilhelm Reich Foundation denied a well-known American author permission to quote extracts from Reich's works in an essay that was, without exception, favorable to the memory and work of Reich.

The trials of the great astronomer Keppler are touched

on in this book. For every Keppler, Galileo, and Nostradamus of the past, there is a Dr. Frances Kelsey in the present. The reader may appreciate some measure of the pressures brought to bear on this modest, tenacious woman when she almost singlehandedly prevented the introduction and circulation of the drug thalidomide into the United States.

Not all successful Borderline personalities are rewarded with adulation. Some are not even blissfully allowed to fade from memory. They must remain on record because of their commitments and accept historical consequences that are often whimsical or ironic:

A woman who had a great vision of equal voting and civil rights for her sex is remembered largely by virtue of having a kind of underwear named after her.

A doctor with a great concern for nutrition and the diet habits of a nation is remembered today only as the inventor of the Graham cracker.

A man who financed the printing and publication of several Borderline movements in America, including phrenology, is best remembered for having spent hundreds of thousands of dollars on an impossible, octagon-shaped house and for having advocated octagonal houses as being the best to promote good health.

A noted advocate of vegetarianism and temperance is remembered as having a wife who sent him out to purchase gin for her and who was given to munching chickens and roasts during her husband's vegetarian meetings.

A pastor of a Protestant sect advocating vegetarianism was so successful in building a new church that he attracted as a next-door neighbor a sausage factory.

A woman noted in her time for being a spiritualist became interested in the vegetarian movement and is now remembered for having felt depressed by the spirits of slaughtered cows when she passed the famed Chicago stockyards.

The Borderline world is not all ghosts and haunts; it is the city of Boston, once having a law against taking baths on its books. It is also visionaries, dreamers, cranks, and frauds. It is Mark Twain, at the peak of his career, afraid to publish an article on mental "telegraphy" because "I feared that the public would treat the thing as a joke and throw it aside, whereas I was in earnest."

Any book presenting a sampling of such people and notions is bound to have out of the ordinary suggestions and theories. Not the least of these in this book is an alleged cure for cancer which involves the eating of Concord grapes or the report of a miraculous stream in North Carolina, whose waters have unexplained curative properties.

Aside from the entertainment and news values of such stories, why do writers who may be otherwise profitably engaged in research or the writing of fiction occupy themselves with the Borderline world?

Mainly, we have these accounts because the writers are impatient with the formalities of science and because they are sincerely interested in helping to expand the boundaries of the known.

Orthodoxy is perhaps the greatest target of Borderline writers and rightly so. It is always when we push the rules to the limit and disregard certain formalities that the potential for freshness and usefulness is increased. The results may well come out silly putty, but to deny the need for silly putty is to deny the need for tomorrow.

To borrow from the critic, Leslie A. Fiedler, this book says "No! in thunder" to the status quo. Fiedler is at great pains to have this *no* understood properly. He quotes Herman Melville, who has written a letter describing the vital force of Nathaniel Hawthorne's artistic abilities:

> There is the grand truth about Nathaniel Hawthorne. He says No! in thunder; but the Devil himself cannot make him say *yes*. For all men who say *yes*, lie; and all men who say *no,*—why, they are in the happy condition of judicious, unencumbered travelers in Europe; they cross frontiers into Eternity with nothing but a carpet-bag . . .

In driving home his point, Mr. Fiedler says Melville's No! in thunder "remains a *no* forever . . . is never partisan; it infuriates Our Side as well as Theirs, reveals that all Sides are one, insofar as they are all yea-sayers and hence all liars."

This book is about aspects of the Borderline world that know how dearest causes are often as likely to be misrepresented as are opposing points of view. It is dedicated to such persons as Dr. Frances Kelsey precisely because of her skepticism and the stand it led her to take on thalidomide. The same skepticism that exposes a crank or a fraud may also expose a chink in the armor of orthodoxy. The same devotion that caused Dr. Sylvester Graham to be remembered only as the "inventor" of a brown cracker made of unbolted wheat will probably cause Dr. Jonas Salk to be remembered for his polio vaccine.

However heartbreaking and ironic it may seem to compare a great vaccine with a Graham cracker, life, itself, is an iffy proposition and no one ever said it was fair or easy.

There are Borderline people among us: quacks, frauds,

visionaries, geniuses, and dreamers. For the same reason that we are uneasy about inexplicable experiences in ourselves, we will probably give these Borderliners comparatively short shrift until they have had their moment and until the time when, and if we can, take them for granted.

—*Shelly Lowenkopf*

THE UNSCIENTIFIC ART OF SUPPRESSION

Joseph F. Goodavage

The scientific establishment seems convinced that the true pioneer performs his job out of some masochistic joy he gets from being rejected and maligned, that he really *wants* to be held up to public ridicule for his efforts.

Nonsense! Science has excluded, ostracized, and damned all those things which have since proven to be the greatest scientific advances. Progress in science is never achieved without the blood, sweat, and tears of lone, dedicated researchers, almost all of whom were suppressed, oppressed, and persecuted for their contributions.

A popular scientific fallacy is that "every real genius is recognized in time. The truth will eventually out."

Not so! Genius is *almost never* recognized for what it is. The inventor or discoverer must first be recognized before he is considered a True Genius. Ostensibly, before recognition, he was an idiot.

A kind of blanket suffocation of ideas goes on all the time by Authorities and Experts who put wrong or stupid opinions into textbooks which stifle the exploration of new avenues of research.

Of course, there's always a risk in trying something new. You face the risk of taking the risk, or the risk of not taking it. Status quo is the more comfortable state of existence. "Let's not rock the boat, boys," quoth Big Science. "We're doing all right as is."

Billions of years of evolution have caused homo sapiens to reign supreme on the planet, mainly because he took chances. Man is the only animal who took the risk of playing with fire. Sure, he lost towns, villages, and cities in the process—lots of people, too. But the benefits far outweighed the risks.

There is always a great risk in breaking with tradition, the old Ritual Taboo Tribal situation. The geographical areas which took these risks moved ahead to become the great nations. Today we see the results of Ritual Taboo Tribal customs among the backward nations of the world.

A deeper look into the reasons behind suppression of new ideas, discoveries, and inventions—the causes of emotional suppression—can stem from economics or simply ultraconservatism due, possibly, to insecurity or neurosis.

Some scientists have fixed ideas about the Fundamental Laws of physics. They hate to change these notions. If an invention, theory, or workable system violates these Laws, even if they are repeatedly demonstrated to work exactly as their originator claims, scientists will rigidly oppose the information rather than change their notions.

Johannes Kepler, a poor teacher of mathematics, saw his wife die, leaving him with a young family. Then his aged mother was thrown into a filthy dungeon for over a year while Kepler fought against insurmountable odds to keep her from being burned to death by the Authorities as a witch.

Yet during this time he managed to evolve his *Mysterium Cosmographicum*, his *Law of Areas*, and, later, his *Laws of Planetary Motion* from which Newton deduced his famous Three Laws of Motion and, we might add, the modern science of astronomy. No astronomer today has made as great a contribution to the general fund of human knowledge.

Kepler's work in astro-meteorology and Newton's astrological writings are *still* being suppressed. Orthodoxy rejects this field without study of evidence because the conventionalists "cannot conceive" how celestial bodies influence weather or earthquakes.

"We condemn astrology from an admittedly uninformed point of view," a Hayden Planetarium astronomer told this writer in 1962.

Alexander Graham Bell was thrown into prison for trying to sell stock in a telephone company. "Utterly ridiculous," they said. "Fraud!" they cried.

When a *theory* says something can't be done, yet the thing *is being done,* the result is often suppression, sometimes quite brutal.

A prominent British physicist had "conclusive mathematical proof" that Edison's incandescent lamp could not possibly work . . . despite the fact that Edison had shown it to work!

(EDITOR'S NOTE: A scientific paper, published by Harvard University "proves" that a bumble bee is aerodynamically unsound and, therefore, unable to fly.)

Out of ignorance, prejudice, jealousy, fear, and ritual tribal taboos, scientific authority has wrecked the lives and careers of our most creative and imaginative fellow creatures. Scorn and ridicule have been visited upon those whom history proved to be real geniuses. They've been thrown into prison, tortured, and even burned alive at the stake for daring to think a new or original thought. Today, we don't burn our heretics. Nevertheless, there are new and more sophisticated forms of suppression.

The literature of science for the past 150 years is full of obscure, ignored, and suppressed evidence that the moon does indeed influence weather, earthquakes, and other natural phenomena. For a century and a half this data was damned by orthodoxy, which displayed a finely discriminating emotional dedication to *the beliefs we now hold.*

The idea of lunar influence is beginning to catch on, but it took a five-year New York University computer study of moon-phase and widespread precipitation to blast a tiny pinpoint of light into orthodoxy's blindness to what should have been a self-evident fact of nature.

In 1930, Forrest Ray Moulton, in his textbook, *Astronomy*, offered this choice morsel of wisdom: "Anyone who knows anything at all about the physics of planetary orbits knows it is impossible to build any sort of interplanetary vessel."

This was a completely gratuitous statement, entirely unnecessary, and, as we now know, completely wrong. But because he was an "Authority" he was read *and believed* by thousands—enough of whom might otherwise have been responsible for a mid-1940s American space technology.

In the September, 1961 issue of *Science*, Dr. Norbert Weiner, the Father of Cybernetics, condemned the majority of young scientists today for refusing even to consider a research project unless it had millions of dollars attached to it. "Stooges in a science factory," he called them, "moppers up" of true originators, he said.

Here's a typical example of what science does to its innovators:

While on the General Hospital Staff in Vienna, Dr. I. P. Semmelweis discovered puerperal fever was an infectious disease and insisted on the antiseptic cleansing of doctors' hands before delivering a baby. His *theory* was completely wrong. He believed the "Odor of Death" on doctors' hands was the cause of childbed fever. In *fact* however, the death rate among Semmelweis' patients dropped from 12 to less than 1 per cent.

His major work, *The Cause, Concept, and Prophylaxis of Childbed Fever,* despite the obvious results of his campaign for scrubbing off the infectious "Odor of Death" from the hands (with chlorinated lime water) was greeted with scorn and ridicule. The fact that he had incriminated obstetricians as the carriers of death (he was right about this, remember) aroused bitter opposition from entrenched authority; the renewal of his position was flatly rejected.

He was driven from Vienna to Budapest but was just as successful there. So successful in fact that the great Medical Authority of the day, Virchow, rallied more opposition against him.

Semmelweis was hounded and persecuted.

He wrote a book called *Etiology.* It was ruthlessly suppressed, yet this book is today recognized as one of the great classics of medical literature.

The suppression turned into a vendetta. Out of sheer desperation, Semmelweis wrote articles denouncing those who rejected his methods as murderers (he was right). Virchow pulled the proper strings; the articles were met by widespread, organized ridicule; Semmelweis was considered insane. His spirit was effectively, ruthlessly, broken. He was thrown into a lunatic asylum and died, ironically enough, from a finger infection incurred during a gynecological operation. He was forty-seven.

It sort of makes you wonder . . .

Dr. Ivy of Krebiozen notoriety is attacked, vilified, held up to ridicule and ruthlessly oppressed by just about all the official Authorities of modern times. Everything you read about this man implies that his sanity is suspect.

It makes you wonder if Dr. Ivy's Krebiozen isn't the real thing after all.

Basic concepts which are now easy for children to grasp—things like the fundamental operation of the solar system—once required the colossal intellectual force of a true genius to conceive when all minds were locked and bound by Dark Age "logic."

At one time, medieval authorities "knew beyond doubt" that the blood could not possibly circulate—as Dr. William Harvey discovered and proved. Everyone "knew" the blood merely ebbed and flowed like the tides of the ocean. Harvey was subjected to ridicule, to persecution and suppression. Today, Medical Authorities are absolutely certain there is no monthly ebb and flow of the blood; it merely circulates "with no appreciable difference" in the rate of pressure or circulation at specific times of the lunar month.

Yet doctors who keep high-objectivity records over periods of years agree that hemorrhaging is more prevalent at the Full Moon than any other time. An increasing number of hospitals recognize this as an unexplained but fundamental fact of nature. More hemostats, plasma, doctors, and nurses are scheduled for Full Moon periods.

Undoubtedly, these hospitals are in a position to save hundreds of lives others would normally lose.

It took twenty years for the idea of the blood's circulation to be generally adopted . . . but only after the *ebb and flow* idea was discarded. The latter is now in disreputable eclipse *despite* factual modern evidence to the contrary.

It is extraordinarily difficult for scientists with preconceived notions to recognize a new, unexpected fact, even when that fact is obvious. Science is the art of making the obvious self-evident.

One of the reasons for this is the fear of nonconformity—of standing out—of being "different." Everyone conforms to group standards for reasons other than fear of punishment. In 1956, Dr. Solomon E. Asch, writing in *Psychological Monographs,* gave a report on a series of "Studies of Independence and Conformity: A Minority of One Against a unanimous Majority."

From three entirely different type colleges, Asch used 123 white male students between ages seventeen and twenty-five. Asch produced a disagreement between an entire group and one individual over a clear and simple fact of eye-witness observation.

All it entailed was the matching of a standard line with one of three comparison lines—all of varying lengths, but one was the same as the standard.

"One by one, students in the unanimous group incorrectly matched the standard with a line *not* its length. Then each dissenting student was asked to state his judgment publicly. Here was pressure to conform."

The erring majority actually succeeded in swaying one-third of the minority judgments. This one-third *denied the clear evidence of their own senses and conformed to the voiced, erroneous majority judgment!*

Some, of course, tried to stick to their guns, but the expressed majority opinion persisted and became stronger as each holdout went down under fire. It was discovered in post-testing interviews that the loners became increasingly self-centered, that they were fearful of being conspicuous or of public exposure of irrelevant "personal defects"—of the approval or disapproval of the group. They were *acutely lonely!*

A few stood up to the challenge. But once their confidence was shaken, a large number of these students yielded; ". . . the presumed rightness of the majority robbed them of the resolution to report and support their own observations. Others who eventually yielded entirely lost sight of the question of accuracy and were solely dominated by a determination not to appear different," Dr. Asch reported.

In other tests the influence of the majority was reduced to nil when it did not voice its collective judgment.

In the *Journal of Social Psychology*, C. H. Marple reported another, similar test: he used control groups as a rigid check on 900 subjects consisting of 300 high school seniors, 300 college seniors, and 300 adults. Each group was given a scale on which to register its opinion on controversial and semi-controversial issues.

The test was repeated after a month. *But before the retesting, all subjects were deliberately informed of the majority opinion on each question.* Result: 64 per cent of high school seniors changed their opinion against 17 per cent for their control group. 55 per cent for the college seniors against 16 per cent for their contol group. Adults: 40 per cent against 14 per cent for *their* control group.

Dr. Marple believes these same percentage results would also apply to a similar test of the entire American population. If so, we can well wonder if there is really such a thing as scientific freedom, individual rights, or a democratic respect for new ideas.

In another area of academic training, our fledgling scientists in high schools, colleges, and universities are known to ignore the results of their own experiments if these results do not concur with what they expect (based upon what they believe the majority wants or anticipates).

The human mind tends to base judgments on its own knowledge, experience, and prejudices rather than on solid facts or new evidence. Often, what passes as scientific fact is instead nothing but superstition. New ideas and discoveries, therefore, are almost always judged in the light of current popular beliefs.

The rejected invention or discovery is one that, for all its intrinsic value, does not jibe with what the Authorities tell the rest of us to believe—even when said Authorities are totally wrong.

Galileo was "too revolutionary." His ideas were too far from the central focus of popular attention. In effect the Inquisitors demanded, "Who are you going to believe— Galileo or us?"

The old astrologer-scientist died blind and broken-hearted under house arrest by the Inquisitors, but Giordano Bruno was burned at the stake in 1600 simply for teaching that the Milky Way is an immense aggregate of suns like our own, with planets revolving around each sun. "Some of these worlds," he said, "are even more glorious than our own . . ."

Discoveries made "before their time" are destined to be

bitterly opposed, fought against with a power usually too strong to be overcome. The utter stupidity of orthodox attitudes was exemplified by the Inquisition when it destroyed Bruno. The joke was really *on them* because the Greeks of classic antiquity had long known the correct explanation for the whiteness of the Milky Way, and *they* had learned it from the Egyptians before them, who got it from the Babylonians and Chaldeans!

We've undergone more than one Dark Age.

Gregor Mendel's brilliant discovery of the basic principles of genetics laid the foundation of an entirely new science, yet it was denounced and damned for thirty-five years after it was published and read before a scientific society.

Mendel was ruthlessly suppressed because another Authority of the Day, one Carl von Nageli of Munich, entertained other theories and "didn't like" Mendel's use of mathematics. After all, who the hell did this insignificant provincial monk think he was? Von Nageli was victimized by his own ego and by his view of himself as a great scientific pundit. Mendel was "a mere amateur expressing fantastic notions."

Other great Authorities of the Day, men of such standing as W. O. Focke, Hermann Hoffman, and Kerner von Marilaun, joined like a pack of wild dogs in the attack on the hapless monk. Today their names don't amount to a tinker's dam, but thanks to these gentlemen, each generation which skimmed through Mendel's paper found only what it was expected to find and ignored anything that didn't conform to its preconceived notions.

Today, ESP is a true suppressed discovery. Orthodox science refuses to soil its sacred robes investigating parapsychology in the manner, say, that biology is studied—yet the two are inseparable.

This borders on the comical because many discoveries of scientists are made *not* through persistent hard research and crucial, controlled experiments, but through a *"sudden flash of insight or illumination."*

Kekule, for example, *dreamed* the atomic structure of the benzene rings. Many scientific problems were solved in dreams.

We may yet learn that *all* new scientific knowledge comes through ESP!

An individual who is outside the "accepted circle" has about a snowball's chance in hell of getting a fair scientific hearing, especially if his fragment of truth lies outside currently prevailing fashions.

Writing in the October 16, 1964, issue of *Science,* astronomer G. C. McVittie of the University of Illinois Observatory said: "I have noticed during my professional lifetime that scientists are much influenced by fashion. There is a tendency to confuse the momentarily fashionable with the fundamental and the significant in science..."

Whether they have any basis in fact or evidence, widely held beliefs develop a kind of spurious validity in scientific minds. Wilfred Trotter of Oxford University said: "... a new idea is the most quickly acting antigen known to science. *If we watch ourselves honestly we shall find that we have begun to argue against a new idea even before it has been completely stated."* (author's italics)

Walsche claims, "The itch to suffocate an infant idea

burns in all of us. Many discoveries have to be made again and again before they are finally accepted."

In his *Scientific Discovery and Logical Proof* F. C. S. Schiller writes that "when a discovery has finally won tardy recognition, it is usually found to have been anticipated, often with cogent reasons and in great detail . . ." Schiller thought this should be counted as one of the Fundamental Laws of Nature.

To the straitjacketed mentalities of some materialistic scientists, anything that doesn't furnish a total solution to a given problem is considered "totally useless."

William I. Beveridge, in *The Art of Scientific Investigation*, writes: "We all know some scientists who steadfastly refuse to be convinced by evidence in support of a discovery which conflicts with their preconceived ideas."

True discoverers, on the other hand, are usually an impatient, undiplomatic, and ill-tempered lot. There is excellent reason for this. They take huge risks and are, by definition, men of great physical and moral courage.

We recognize the courage of men like Harvey, Jenner, Semmelweis, and Pasteur in the face of powerful opposition, but what about the thousands of discoverers who lacked their intestinal fortitude? How many lines of profitable investigation have been killed due to opposition by Scientific Authority?

Here's an example:

In 1845, about the time Semmelweis started his campaign for antisepsis in hospitals, J. J. Waterston wrote a scientific paper on the molecular theory of gases in which he anticipated the work of Joule, Clerk Maxwell, and Clausius. The referee of the Royal Society to whom it was presented sneered, "this paper is nothing but nonsense."

That broke Dr. Waterston. His work lay in disrepute

for nearly a half century during which he lived in broken-hearted obscurity. Then mysteriously, without a trace, he disappeared.

In 1925 an obscure science teacher was prosecuted for teaching evolution in the notorious "Tennessee Monkey Trial."

Thirty years afterward, super-scholar Immanuel Velikovsky was savagely attacked by the scientific community for suggesting, among other things, that the idea of Darwin's evolutionary theory and Lyall's Uniformism might have a few glaring flaws. He went so far as to build a towering structure of facts and evidence to support his contentions.

Without examining his evidence, orthodoxy bitterly damned Velikovsky. He had committed the unpardonable sin of writing popular books for laymen rather than submitting papers to the accepted scientific groups—papers which would then have gathered the dust of decades in obscure university vaults.

Velikovsky stands or falls on his evidence. A dozen years after he had anticipated the mean temperature and chemical composition of the atmosphere of Venus, *Mariner* II proved him 100 per cent right with all its telemetered data. Everything Mariner discovered, Velikovsky had predicted.

But are his former detractors now convinced? Are they swayed by the facts? Not a bit; they hate him all the more for having shown them to be damned fools.

The evolution of any original idea can be divided into three phases: (a) at first it is ridiculed, called "impossible," "a fantasy," or "useless"; (b) years or decades later, the "experts" concede it may have some merit, but that it would never be of any practical use; and finally (c) when the idea or discovery is favored with general acclaim, its former critics and attackers either say they've "known it all along," or, "there's nothing really original about it. After all, it's been anticipated by others."

"Nothing can possibly be a panacea for all known minor ailments. That's snake oil talk," says the modern medic.

Let's see . . . ninety-seven years ago, a chemical solvent called dimethyl sulphoxide was synthesized in Germany from leftovers from the paper manufacturing process. DMSO, as it is now called, is a fantastic new experimental drug in America, but no mention is made of the fact that poor Germans were using it for decades prior to World War I. DMSO, it seems, cures arthritis, sinusitis, headaches, earaches, sprains, and burns. It reduces swellings, suppresses blisters, kills pain, tranquilizes, fights germs, enhances the action of other drugs, and may be injected, swallowed, rubbed on, or dripped in.

A short preliminary paper on its effects was published in February, 1964. True to "scientific" form, the paper was immediately attacked as "The most preposterous article ever to appear in the medical literature!"

Maybe so, but the University of Oregon Medical School and Crown Zellerbach Corp., the second largest paper producer in America, have joined forces to put DMSO across.

Anyone who really thinks about it and looks hard enough will find dozens of genuine discoveries and inventions being suppressed.

Take cancer cures, for example. Hundreds of thousands of Americans die of cancer. Drugs, surgery, and radiation seem to have no effect whatever on the course

28

of this dread disease. Yet when *unorthodox* remedies result in cures, the evidence is casually dismissed with something like, "Oh, that proves nothing. Cancers often disappear for no known reason. Spontaneous regression, you know."

Funny thing about "spontaneous regression." It's never mentioned when a doctor diagnoses a patient's illness as cancer, treats him, and then the patient happens to recover! The fact is that many people who have been told they had cancer later found the diagnosis completely wrong.

Yet we've been pouring tens of millions of dollars in contribution in a War Against Cancer for a couple of decades now. What happens to all the money collected during these ever-bigger-and-bigger fund drives?

Krebiozen seems to have saved the lives of thousands.

Krebiozen is suppressed. *Dr. Ivy's sanity is challenged!* Here is a man who was recognized universally as a medical super-high-power genius, a man who was given every conceivable honor the medical fraternity could bestow upon one of its brilliant stars . . . *until he started saving lives with Krebiozen!*

Mucorihicin, a yeast mold derivative made in Pittsburgh, Pa., was effective in saving additional thousands of cancer-sufferers—nearly 100 per cent of whom were formerly given up as "hopeless."

Is it coincidental that those who recovered had taken Mucorihicin . . . or were they all simply cases of "spontaneous regression"?

You can't get Mucorihicin any more. It is suppressed in this country by the Federal Drug Administration and attacked by the American Medical Association.

Yet millions of dollars were once offered for rights to

the formula by several big drug companies. Nutrition Service, Inc., turned down these generous offers on purely humanitarian grounds. The Big Guys wanted to price it beyond the reach of those who need it most.

The effectiveness of cancer treatment is inversely proportionate to their cost. You need about $7,000 to pay for the orthodox treatments before you die of the disease—unless you're a charity case or are heavily insured. This doesn't count funeral costs.

Or . . . you can treat yourself at home for about $20 with a high probability of recovering completely. This is what a breakfast of Concord grapes or the unadulterated juice thereof will cost for a two- or three-month period.

According to the testimonials of over 200 ex-cancer sufferers compiled by John Irons of Albany, Ga., *pure unsweetened Concord grape juice has cured all of them!*

Almost ninety years old, Irons is tough-minded, literate, and dedicated to the proposition that people have a right to try anything at all when they're faced with the prospect of bankruptcy and death by orthodox medical treatments. He spent decades searching for simple home remedies and off-beat cures for just about every ailment under the sun. He cured himself of arthritis and a near-fatal cancer of the colon. He has cured all but two cases of cancer by passing on the information he had gathered to anybody who asks for it. The two failures were so advanced that they couldn't have survived long enough to try the grape treatment.

The American Medical Association and the Food and Drug Administration would like to string the old buzzard from the nearest flagpole. They're powerless, of course, because he is selling absolutely nothing, just telling people how to cure themselves of everything from colds to cancer.

It is, of course, "outrageous . . . unpardonable . . . quackery . . ." and what-have-you. So far, Irons had not consented to kindly keel over and die, thank you.

"I sat me down," Irons said, "and figured the golden harvest reaped from the unfortunate victims of malignancy. They do not cure, do not mean to cure, but string them along for months, years if they last that long, treating them only with sedative pills. When the end is near the victim is sent home to die, as an incurable 'terminal'. I found that with those treated in regular orthodox manner, the harvest is nearly $78 million per month, not year but month. The average 'take' from a lingering cancer victim is $7,000, from him and his relatives. Check up on a few and see if this is not correct. Even that could be forgiven, if they cured. In seven years I have not found one genuine internal cancer cured by the regular orthodox treatment. Have found a number cured by Quacks and have seen those quacks put out of business by legal persecution. Also I have found eight cancer cures, seven of them known to A.M.A., but suppressed. That $7,000 plus (have known it to reach $10,000) shrivels the oath of Hippocrates, and all humane instincts . . ."

This writer has personally observed the regression of three cases of cancer via the grape treatment where neither surgery nor radiation did any good.

If the Concord grape treatment for malignancy is as effective as it appears to be, why isn't it fully investigated by fair and impartial methods and the results announced publicly?

Medical Authorities might have a difficult time convincing people that grape juice is harmful.

Over in England there's a ten-foot tall electrical space engine called the Vortella. It seems to be the answer to a spaceman's dream. Its potential for getting man to the planets and beyond is everything its developers claim.

The April, 1964, issue of *Uranus,* a British scientific and technological publication, carried a complete report on the Vortella Project, adding: "As could be expected, such a scientific breakthrough has met with but a cold reception from the pundits, who are unwilling to admit that it is only their ignorance of basic scientific principles which prevented them from inventing it themselves."

The United States Weather Bureau and American Meteorological Society are guilty of the same sort of reactionary attitude. Practically all USWB personnel are civil service employees and members of the AMS. The Bureau spends almost 200 million dollars each year— fifty million of this is channeled into the search for some way of making accurate long-range weather predictions.

We-l-l-l, along comes this astro-meteorologist who, with paper and pencil and several weeks of mathematical calculations, sits down and out-predicts the entire mighty United States Weather Bureau on long-range weather forecasts. He doesn't concern himself with average temperatures and rainfalls. He tells you where and when the blizzards, floods, droughts, hurricanes, and tornadoes will strike.

What's more, a pre-published series of crucial experiments by G. J. McCormack of Fair Lawn, N.J., proved astro-meteorology to be 94 per cent accurate on the average during a six-month period during which rigid control conditions were used.

Only after political pressure was brought to bear on the Chief of the Weather Bureau was a formal hearing of McCormack's *Theory and Practice of Astronomic Weather Forecasting* arranged in the New York Bureau's offices. It was later presented to the 44th Annual meeting of the American Meteorological Society early in 1964.

And when McCormack's far-in-advance predictions worked out with unerring accuracy, who came forward to apologize for rejecting the system? Who wanted to put the USWB or the AMS officially behind a full investigation of how the planets cause our weather?

Nobody, that's who. Fifty million dollars *each year* is being siphoned off for the development of a long-range weather forecasting system. Once it is found, no more fifty million.

McCormack has furnished his forecasts at a profit to industry, farmers, and entire municipalities in thirty-six states. His one mistake seems to have been misguided idealism. When he retired from active forecasting in 1951, he wanted to give his system to the government weather bureau, *gratis*.

They'll have none of it.

The lesson of history is obvious. If you happen to make a revolutionary new discovery or invention, don't expect to bask in the approbation of Big Science. Figure out some way to make a lot of money with it. Oh, they'll call you a crackpot, a fraud, and a quack. We all do this— scientist and layman alike.

And it'll hurt you deeply.

You'll probably cry all the way to the bank.

Joseph S. Hufham

About twenty-six years ago I took a day off to go fishing. I had more than the average fisherman's luck. I was instantly healed of a severe, baffling eye disease.

About two years prior, I'd contracted an eye ailment. My eyes became "raw" red, and quite painful. Dr. Slade Smith, of Whiteville, North Carolina, examined my eyes, prescribed glasses and drops. By the time the prescribed glasses arrived they were of little benefit.

Pain was so great that at times I used vapor or rubbing alcohol for a few moments' respite. Two years passed and my doctor's prescriptions failed to bring the disease under control. That's when I took a day off for fishing.

A revival meeting was being held in our community church and it was suggested that I have my eyes prayed for. I did. The evangelist asked the elders of the church to lay hands upon me according to the Bible. They anointed me with oil and prayed, but I felt no healing touch. However, as the English poet William Cowper said, "God works in mysterious ways His wonders to perform."

The evangelist spent the night with me and the next

morning we went to a place called Windy Point, which is where Shallotte Inlet, Brunswick county, southeastern North Carolina, empties into the Intracoastal Waterway. The sun was so bright on the water it pained my eyes, trying to see how to bait my hook.

Determined to get fun out of the trip anyway, I dove in for a swim. My eyes smarted as I went down. I figured it was just the salt in the water. But as I bobbed up I found that I could look at the sun without feeling one iota of pain. Just like that, I'd received my cure.

I was doing a column for *The News Reporter,* published at Whiteville, N.C., and so I made casual mention of my cure.

In April, 1963, I retired from business and decided I'd do a full column on my cure which had held good all those twenty-odd years. Curious readers went to the stream, and soon they were reporting miraculous cures. It was about this time that J. B. Bordeaux, a farmer of Delco rural, experienced a baffling rash. He was swollen across the chest, under his arms, and was bleeding from pea-size bumps from his wrists up to his armpits.

In the early spring of 1963 Dr. J. N. Dawson, plant physician for the Riegel Paper Company, at Riegelwood, and presently president of the Columbus County Cancer Society, treated Bordeaux for poison ivy, and Bordeaux responded to the treatment nicely, all signs drying away.

In July following, however, Bordeaux broke out with this baffling rash and went to Dr. Dawson for treatment. This time he did not respond, and so the doctor suggested a skin specialist. Instead, having read of others being healed by the "miracle" water from Shallotte Inlet, Bordeaux used a teacupful of the water to wet the afflicted area, and what happened was astonishing.

By morning the bumps had dried up, the bleeding had stopped, the pain and redness and swelling were gone, and within four days the skin breaks had healed. Learning of this, Dr. Dawson called to see this writer, removed his own glasses, put a drop of the water into each eye, and within five minutes picked up a magazine and began reading small print.

He was so astonished he agreed to go with this writer to Shallotte, and a few days later we toured the stream in a small motorboat. We brought under suspicion an estimated 16 square miles of a unique grass feeding something we believed to be tremendously antibiotic into the water. This led to more newspaper reports and more cures.

Jesse Shaw, a rural Riegelwood farmer, was cured of a rusty spike wound at one wading. He'd obtained a gash from a rusty nail years prior, while stepping off a farm-cart. Shaw said he'd been able to get the bone-deep wound in the calf of his leg to scab over, but pus had formed beneath. He'd tried numerous antiseptics, he said, but they had lacked the penetrating power of the miracle water.

Little eighteen-month-old Keith Lewis, of Supply, whose home is a few miles from the stream, was cured of a blocked nasal duct. The child's mother, Mrs. Toby Lewis, told this reporter: "Keith was born with the blocked nasal duct and he kept his eye rubbed red. Our family doctor was unable to get the eye to respond to treatment and so he suggested that I see an eye specialist."

Mrs. Lewis said the specialist agreed to undertake

opening the nasal duct by running a probe down the inner corner of the eye. "But we read of how your eyes were healed by use of the Inlet Water," she said, "so I decided to give the water a chance."

In giving this testimony to us for publication, Mrs. Lewis added, "It took about twenty drops of the water—a drop or two a day over a period of two weeks—to completely open the nasal duct and cure the child."

Fifteen-month-old Stanley Edward Furlough, of Riegelwood, was cured of a disease other treatments had failed on. The child, his mother said, was born with a fungus that looked as if it would "cut both ears off." In giving this testimony for publication, Mrs. Furlough said:

"I've tried almost all kinds of antiseptics trying to effect a cure of the child's ears. A baby specialist tried, effected no cure; and once I had Stanley Edward hospitalized. Still, no cure. I hadn't read of the miracle water's curative power, but I'd heard so much talk about it my husband and I decided to try a little on our baby's ears. The first application, just a drop or so, came near doing the job, but one little place of infection about the size of a grain of rice, was left. One drop of the water on that finished off the job, effecting a complete cure."

Numerous other cures have been effected. One of the outstanding was that of skin cancers. George Wooten, retired, of Riegelwood, had been receiving specialized treatment for recurring skin cancers over a period of ten years. About eighteen months ago he went to a place called "Gause Landing" near where Shallotte Inlet empties into the Intracoastal Waterway. He had four cancers; three on his face, one on his arm. His wife had one on her left cheek. After applying the water each day over a period of five days, the scabs were off and new skin formed, closing the previously affected areas.

Dr. C. L. Wooten, retired, of Whiteville, gave his testimony by phone to the society editor of *The News Reporter* for this writer to publish. Dr. Wooten was afflicted twenty years ago with a baffling rash on top of his feet. He went to Duke hospital where doctors told him it varied in appearance from athlete's foot disease only in that it was on top of his feet instead of between his toes.

Dr. Wooten did not receive his cure at the hospital. A few days later he went on vacation to Cresent Beach, waded, and was cured. Water flowing from Shallotte Inlet goes the way of Cresent beach. The doctor says that the ailment has never given him any more trouble.

One reader of this writer's newspaper column, after reading of numerous cures effected by the miracle water, phoned in with the suggestion that dimethyl sulfoxide, used by the Riegel Paper Company, at their Riegelwood plant, was flowing down Cape Fear river to Shallotte (about 60 miles) and enhancing the curative power of the Inlet Water.

A check with one of Riegel's leading chemists brought an assurance that no dimethyl sulfoxide was being let into the river. This writer experimented with some of the miracle water on a badly scalded thumb, found that it quickly eased the pain, and that it revitalized the under skin so that it reseated itself. Whereupon he wrote President Johnson that in the event of a nuclear war the water could be used as a strong antibiotic to combat infection.

A few days later this writer received a letter from the Department of the Army which said in part:

"Be assured that we are anxious to learn of each new

development that offers hope of more effectively relieving suffering and aiding in national recovery following a nuclear attack. Upon receipt of corroborative scientific and medical evidence, we shall certainly take whatever action is necessary best to use these waters."

This writer has written and received responsive letters also from: American Cancer Society, Leonard Wood Memorial for the eradication of leprosy, the American Medical Association, and from the North Carolina Board of Pharmacy, some offering suggestions, some wishing Dr. Dawson and me luck.

We have indirectly contacted leading American laboratories and have learned that the production of a good antibiotic can very well cost up to a million dollars, and that private drug companies are reluctant to invest so much to test and properly evolve a drug unless there is a chance of a monopoly that will somewhat guarantee them an opportunity to get their money back.

In the case of the water around Shallotte there is little chance of a private company getting a monopoly on it. The area is large, and the channel is owned by the U.S. government. Therefore it is free to the public, and since our discovery has received widespread publicity this writer knows that water from the Inlet has been hauled away by carloads to as far north as Connecticut, and as far south as Florida, and testimonies of cures have come in over a wide area.

Dr. Dawson had competent chemists analyze some of the water and told this reporter that nothing harmful was found in it, and that it would not be damaging to inform the public.

Experimenting, this writer has found that juice from

raw oysters taken from the inlet has renewed strength to tired eyes. Folk living near the area, especially Holden Beach and Ocean Isle fishermen, report that it has "been known for ages" that the water would cure up "the worst kind of sores," and now folk are wondering if it isn't the stream the Indians told Ponce de Leon about.

Carl Payne Tobey

Although the first psychologists were probably the ancient astrologers who delineated twelve basic types of personality traits, there is no such thing as a pure personality in astrology. This would call for a person who was born with all the planets in the same sign of the zodiac.

There is neither record nor likelihood of this phenomenon ever happening. But there is strong likelihood of new, workable information which will have a direct bearing on the interpretation of the personality of any individual, regardless of birth date. This information comes from research, observation, and investigation focused on three signs of the zodiac grouped together as the Water signs.

All the ancient civilizations which left traces of astrology development behind them also left a similar set of symbols as well. These ancients divided the space around the earth into twelve equal parts, then into 144 equal parts.

There is absolutely nothing out in space or in the fixed stars that could conveniently accept division into either twelve or 144 equal parts, giving clear indications, then, that the divisions of signs were made mathematically in whatever civilization astrology played a part. The zodiacs in the Americas were divided in the same way as those in Europe, Africa, or India, and the symbols bore a marked similarity. Gemini was always represented by two people, Sagittarius with arrows, Taurus with husky animals, Cancer with seashells, Pisces with fish, etc.

The twelve signs of the zodiac have been divided into four trinities which have been described as Fire (the vital), Earth (the physical), Air (the intellectual), and Water (the emotional).

This is rather common knowledge, readily available to followers of astrology, but what follows is based on theories of a New York physician and the research of this writer, which includes more than thirty years of intensive interviewing to confirm or deny the results of interpreting horoscopes.

The Water signs are Scorpio (born October 23–November 21), Pisces (born February 19–March 20), and Cancer (born June 23–July 22).

Scorpio has been associated with the sexual side of the personality, but Dr. Wilbur E. Worden, an Ithaca, N. Y. physician, was the first person to point out that there was more to this, that another Water sign, Pisces, also has a relationship to sex. It was his first reaction that Scorpio represented the male principle in sex while Pisces represented the female principle. This led the present writer to speculating. If two of the Water signs are associated with the sexual nature, what about the third, Cancer?

The results of the speculation will be treated in informal essays on each of the three signs in the Water trinity, and depending on the positions of one or all of these signs in the individual's horoscope, may be used accordingly to give a more sophisticated and dimensional reading to any chart. The information is not limited to those who are, by birth, a Scorpion, a Piscean, or a Cancerian, and should be treated accordingly.

SCORPIO

Scorpio represents hereditary factors and family survival. It is accompanied by loyalty to the family, to the ancestors. This is an unconscious loyalty. To Scorpio, there are insiders and outsiders. Blood relatives are insiders. All others are outsiders. Scorpio may hate his brother, but he will fight beside his brother if an outsider is involved. If we could have people who were 100 per cent Scorpio, the only form sex could take would be incest. Even without 100 per cent, we still have some incest, much more than the majority of us assume. Authorities state that the majority of rape cases are not reported because they would involve family embarrassment. They refer to cases of statutory rape, where the girl is a willing party but is under eighteen. These authorities in police departments tell us that the man is usually the father, the brother, or the uncle of the girl, which is why the matter is not reported. These statistics were taken from a television broadcast by the University of Arizona.

Next to incest is the common case of the girl who has a romance with, or marries, a man who resembles her father. Noting how often a member of the opposite sex had told the writer that he looked like her father, we asked other men about this, and we found few men who had not attracted women who stated that they looked like the male parent. Most of these women would be horrified if they realized they were disclosing their own unconscious desire for incest, yet it is there. It is always around.

In its extreme form, Scorpio is also the sadist. When sexually aroused, Scorpio can be cruel. There is a sexual reaction at seeing pain inflicted on others, and sometimes to have it inflicted upon oneself. Children who are habitually beaten and abused by adults and schoolteachers sometimes escape the pain by having sex reactions. This is one reason why corporal punishment should not be tolerated in schools. There is also the possibility that the teacher is gaining sexual satisfaction from abusing the child. As a sex partner, Scorpio is likely to be seeking relief, and for that reason is interested exclusively in self-satisfaction without regard to the interests of the partner.

Where the Scorpio factor is not radical, manifestation can be in milder forms. The Scorpio employee is loyal to the firm employing his services. Again, there are insiders and outsiders. People who work for the firm are the insiders. They are part of the organization. All other people, including the customers, are actually regarded as outsiders. They are to be catered to if they are customers, but they are still regarded as outsiders. An employer can trust his Scorpio employees. They are all for the boss. There is extreme loyalty to one's fraternity, to one's political party, to one's country.

Although this is one of the most sexual signs of the zodiac, it is also the sign of the guilt complex. This is the girl who is so passionate until the act is over, and who then bursts out in tears. Scorpio can be unscrupulous and then remorseful. It is the first to offend, the first to apologize. This sign was on the eastern horizon when Dr. Sigmund Freud was born. His greatest sex problem was within himself, and he saw his own problems reflected in every patient. The evangelists who preach against sex as sin are most likely to be the Scorpio type. They are fighting sin, not in the outside world, but in themselves. The sin they see everywhere is within themselves. They carry it wherever they go. They can't get away from it. Billy Sunday was Sun-in-Scorpio. So is Billy Graham. Another evangelist, out preaching against sin and sex, consulted the writer as a client with a problem. It was a sex problem. He put it this way, "In my position, I can't just go out and play the field."

It is a paradox, but despite the sex drive of Scorpio, this is the sign that associates Scorpio with sin. For some reason, Scorpio can't get away from the idea that sex is wrong. He can't relax. Perhaps this is because, with these people, sex and violence go together. They can't seem to separate the two. Scorpio, in an effort to be virtuous and at one with God, will attempt abstinence, but this only causes the sex factor to build up, and the greater the buildup the more it can become associated with violence. Under the strain, the person may perform a violent act, and then suffer violently from the guilt. These are the people who often want the strictest sex rules accompanied by punishment for violation of the rules. Perhaps they enjoy punishing and being punished. Perhaps this is some kind of a throwback. We have often noted that such people will sometimes relive the design of an ancestor, do some very unusual things that an ancestor did, without ever having heard about that ancestor, and without any knowledge or consciousness that the behavior of the ancestor is being repeated.

PISCES

Pisces is every bit as sexual as Scorpio, but in a completely different way. There is no sense of guilt. Pisces likes sex and is not likely to be hypocritical about it. Pisces likes nudity, and is not self-conscious about it. It is the natural state. There is a love of the feeling of air on the skin. Rules, laws, and regulations are taboo. Because it believes in the natural, and because it does not believe in restrictions, Pisces likes the illicit. There is a greater thrill if it is illicit. To Pisces, promiscuity is also natural. This is also a sign of sympathy and compassion. It is more the masochist than the sadist. There is no cruelty. Instead of the self-satisfaction of Scorpio, here we find that pleasure comes from satisfying the other person. Almost anything about sex is a pleasure to Pisces if it does not involve pain. This sign does not want to see anyone hurt. In a collection of the birth data of prostitutes, this sign rated at the top, with the low exactly opposite it in the sign Virgo, which means *the virgin*. To Pisces, there is no sin involved in sex. The sign is always sympathetic to the underdog, and this has often been described as a characteristic of prostitutes.

Even the most ancient of the ancients portrayed Scorpio as jealous, but Pisces is not usually so inclined. The Pisces person is least likely to resent the marital partner having an outside partner. It may even be encouraged. Sex is more likely to be looked upon as one of the luxuries of life rather than as any sin. Yet, it likes the trimmings, all the things that will increase the allure. Most psychologists have this factor strong somewhere in a chart. The sign is not noted for truthfulness. It believes in happiness, and if illusions contribute to happiness, it believes in illusions. It colors everything in order to conceal or beautify anything that may be ugly. Pisces can absorb liquor, but is least likely to become an alcoholic. On the other hand, Scorpio is probably most likely to become an alcoholic, but there is that guilt complex.

Something in the nature of these people causes them to be sexually attracted to their social inferiors. We see it particularly in girls who are born into wealthy families. There may be an affair with a servant. There is that feeling that by making themselves sexually available they are doing some good in the world. They are often caught up in scandal, because what is right and natural to them is scandalous to others. Their lives are often ruined because of their sympathetic association with unreliable people. Pisces sees nothing wrong with adultery, because Pisces makes no associations between customs and morality. To this sign, all promiscuity is natural, and there is that belief that nature intended it that way. Sex is no more to be banned or restricted than any other luxury.

One Pisces woman told us that she would like to have five husbands, and bragged that she could take care of all of them every night. Upon reading these characteristics, another Pisces woman asked, "Just why am I like that? The first week I was married, I went to bed with the milk man."

Incest is definitely not a characteristic of Pisces. The sign is inclined toward the general principles of socialism.

There is no prejudice against other races. In fact, there is curiosity about them, including sexual curiosity. There is the desire to overcome poverty for all, and that includes sexual poverty. There is no looking down on others. Accompanying these characteristics, we find enthusiasm, inspiration, idealism, and many illusions. Crime is not recognized as such. It is considered an illness. The criminal is to be pitied rather than punished. In carrying out such ideals, these people usually suffer because they are exploited.

The ancients also associated this sign with the feet, with dancing, with rhythm. Statistics indicate it as a top sign among musicians. In many ways, it is the most mysterious of all signs. Often, we find these people most successful in advertising and public relations jobs. They make good actors and actresses. Elizabeth Taylor is an example, Jean Harlow another. On the other hand, there was Luther Burbank, who talked to his flowers and claimed they responded to affection with better health.

With their idealism, often regarded by others as impractical, crackpot idealism, these people suffer from much mental and emotional confusion. They have intervals when they do not know what they want, and they are the most susceptible to nervous breakdowns and mental illness. They may often appear to be taking life very easy, when things are boiling far beneath the surface. They do not follow the rules, in which they do not believe, and they often suffer for it. This is the Greenwich Village type and the artist. This is a design.

We do not know why we find these different characteristics together, but physicists do not know why they find certain elements together, nor do mathematicians know why prime numbers follow the design they do.

Pisces feels for the other person, cannot bear to see others in pain, must help. This is one great difference between Pisces and Scorpio, but the other great difference is that Pisces has no feeling of guilt.

CANCER

When Dr. Worden first came forth with the concept that sex was not confined to Scorpio, and that it was as much represented by Pisces, the idea was so contrary to the general belief of modern astrologers that we set out to prove him wrong, but the more we investigated, the more evidence that he was right piled up. It was sex, but it was different. That left a big question. If two of the Water trinity signs were to be associated with sex, what about Cancer, the third such sign? We could see no connection.

The writer has taught astrology as a mathematical set of principles to nearly 700 people over the country and a few in foreign countries. Letters were sent out to the best students. We wanted to see whether the students could see what we couldn't see. Occasionally, a hint came from here or there, but the evidence was not building up rapidly. From a sex viewpoint, the sign seemed hard to penetrate. After six years of exploring, the evidence is still not clear. Yet, there does seem to be a connection. The evidence is well covered most of the time because of an element of hypocrisy.

There is a front. Cancer pretends to be what it isn't. This sign wants to be practical. In that connection, birth dates of people listed in *Who's Who in Commerce and Industry* show this to be the most successful of the signs

49

in making money. These are usually successful people in business. Money comes first. Women of this sign are coy. Perhaps the men are, too. They are not outspoken. These people do not respond to questions of the researcher in the same manner that Scorpio or Pisces does. Realizing that the intimate questions of the investigator are merely an effort to reach deeper truths, either Scorpio or Pisces will spill the details in order to help. Not Cancer. He is on the defensive and retreats into his shell. The ancient symbol for the sign in Europe and Africa was the crab, but elsewhere, it was always the shellfish of some variety.

Through direct questioning as well as careful observation, we have tried to find out more about these people. We find that Cancer is often the girl who gets raped. She makes sure of it. She likes to get raped. In that way, she maintains her innocence, and she can use it against her companion. She can blackmail him a little in a nice sort of way. She will overlook it for a price.

Cancer is the introvert, and it is difficult to dig inside and see what is going on. There is marked insecurity and a lack of self-confidence. There is a feeling of weakness which must be compensated. Remember that the men are the most successful in business. The woman has a natural business sense, too. When propositioned, she is indignant, but not too indignant. She doesn't run away. She sticks around, but she isn't *that* kind of a girl. She would never have sex with a man unless married to him, but she seems willing to trade and barter a little. Much depends on the price, flowers, clothes, a better job, even money maybe.

Note the odd physical and biological associations of the ancients. They associated Scorpio with the sex organs,

Pisces with the feet, and Cancer with the breasts. On the average, Cancer women have more prominent breasts. Although the public merely associates the zodiacal signs with the seasons of the year, the zodiacal sign on the eastern horizon or ascendent is more important. These girls are well-rounded. They are not likely to be tall. They have curves. They look very female. There is that baby face. They seem so innocent. At least in personal appearance, this is the motherly type. It seeks the very masculine counterpart. Even the men are likely to be more on the effeminate side. You have the feeling that you want to protect these people. They act like babies.

A prominent district attorney said that he was always fearful of prosecuting a rape case. He found it difficult to be sure that it was rape. He told us of a case involving a Cancer woman. A man had been in jail for some time, awaiting his trial on rape charges. He was accused of kidnaping a young housewife, taking her out on the desert and raping her. Assistants in the D.A's. office had been very thorough in their investigation. The trial date had been set. Finally, the D.A. sat down and studied all the reports. He said he did not want to go ahead with the case until he had talked with the victim. She was brought to his office. He interviewed her alone. The story seemed to hold together, but he had an uncertain feeling. He went over her story a number of times.

Finally, he said, "What did he do when this was all over? Did he leave you out there on the desert? Did he drive you back to town, or did you have to walk home? Just what did he do when it was all over?"

By now, feeling the strain, the girl said, "Well, first, we stopped off for coffee."

This was the first break. Now, the questioning grew

more intense. In a little while, the girl broke down and told the true story. Her husband was out of town. She had picked the man up at a bar, had driven out on the desert with him and had willingly had sexual relations with him. She arrived home at four in the morning and discovered that her husband had unexpectedly returned. She could think of no legitimate explanation for coming home at 4:00 A.M., or for where she had been. She panicked. She told her husband the story about being kidnaped. He phoned the police. It all happened so fast. The man was picked up, charged with rape. He would have been on his way to prison had the district attorney not been the type who always had doubts about a rape case.

Evangeline Adams, the famed astrologer, said she found more prostitutes under Cancer than any other sign. This does not conform with other statistics, but perhaps because this is the *respectable* prostitute. You don't find her in the red-light district. She is not cheap. In fact, she can be damned expensive, most expensive of all.

If Cancer men are the most successful in business, and statistics indicate they are, Cancer women are the most successful in the business of sex. They intend to better themselves. A good marriage to a money-making partner is of first consideration. If that is not immediately forthcoming, a girl has to get along meanwhile. Marriage is a means toward financial security, and these girls want as much security as they can get. They want good friends, and they regard diamonds as good friends.

These girls have a weakness. You can get at the truth if you appeal to this weakness. Within themselves, they are very proud of their accomplishments. With their baby ways, they still mother their men. They calculate men's weaknesses. If you go about it right, you can trap them into bragging about their sexual accomplishments. To them, making a profit out of the weaknesses of men is evidence of their superior intelligence. These people are not intellectual. They are down-to-earth, practical people. They value material success. They accumulate material things. They accumulate money. They hoard it and hide it away. They are prepared for the rainy day when it comes. The husband of a Cancer girl will never know what she has hidden away, but when everything goes wrong, when he is dead broke and despondent, the wife will always turn up with what he needs to start over again.

We questioned a Cancer girl in her late twenties. We had broken through some of her armour. She was married to an attorney. She had two lovely children, and a maid to look after them on special occasions. She was a highly respected mother in the community. Finally, we touched her weak spot. She bragged. She was a very beautiful motherly type. With a cold attitude toward her husband, she explained that he was an instrument.

"I want money. He is going to be very successful. He will get it for me. I can do anything I want to with him. I can make him successful. He will get me anything I want. I'm going to make him successful, and I'm going to have fun too."

She was very proud of her "intelligent" methods of managing things. In her own community, she was the most virtuous of the virtuous, but she took a day off every week. She went to another town where she knew no one.

53

She met men at bars. She went to bed with them. She had "fun too." These girls are very proud of their accomplishments, and when they feel safe in doing so, they will brag.

Just as the men are ever concentrating on a profit in business, Cancer women are always concentrating on a profit from sex. None of this even trade business. That is foolish. There must be a profit. Cancer is going to trade and barter before there is any sex act. The trading over, agreement reached, the business end of things concluded, here is a man's most passionate companion, but she is never passionate at home. She would never allow her husband to think she enjoys sex. She is putting herself out just for him. He must never think she enjoys it. That would be bad business on her part. She is never guilty of bad business methods. When her husband has to entertain business friends, here is the perfect hostess. She will be a distinct asset to her husband. She will do everything right, and he will be very proud of her. With her husband, she never overcomes her timidity. She won't want him to see her completely in the nude, but with a stranger, she can strip off her clothes and have no inhibitions. Few friends or acquaintances of this girl ever get to know her. She is smart, and she is shrewd. She isn't about to reveal herself. What her friends and her husband see is another person she has created just for them. Her whole revealed personality is a front. She is the motherly little breast girl all men feel it their duty to protect.

As a whole, the Water trinity represents three survival dynamics. It is important to realize that these are principles of nature. The individuals are seldom actually conscious of why they do something or think what they do. Scorpio does not know why sex and cruelty are associated in his nature. Pisces does not know why it is necessary to help the weak. Cancer does not know why it follows a certain pattern or design, why it is necessary to be hypocritical. Cancer represents the Individual Survival dynamic, Scorpio the Family Survival dynamic, and Pisces the Social Survival dynamic. For Cancer, sex is employed for personal survival and profit. Scorpio is driven to sex for family survival. Heredity can't continue without children, and there can't be children without sex. Experience seems to indicate that more Scorpio teenage girls get pregnant before marriage than girls of any other sign. This would appear to be due to the fact that when the moment comes, they are too driven to take precautions. A married woman in her thirties, with two children, became pregnant by a foreign student. We asked her why she took no precautions. She said, "I don't know. I had my diaphragm with me. I guess I just didn't want to delay it."

Study those three ancient symbols and study these three types of people. We have stated that Cancer puts up a front. Literally, the Cancer woman has a front in those breasts, but she was represented by the crab that lived in a shell. Scorpio was associated with the male sex organs. The symbol was the scorpion, but sometimes an eagle to portray a more noble side. It is interesting to note that the scorpion was employed as a symbol on both sides of the Atlantic long before the white man came to the western hemisphere. Pisces is associated with the sea and potential Neptunian influences, but it is also closely linked with the feet. It is from this latter association that we make the relationship between feet and dancing. There have been clearly defined relationships made between dancing and sexual activity, and on a primitive level, dancing serves important ceremonial and presexual functions. With some primitive tribes, dancing is a means of inducing orgiastic abandonment prior to ritual sex relations. This would have a strong appeal to the Piscean or an individual with a Pisces influence in his sexual nature.

Henry J. Santon

Escaping the steaming heat of Acapulco, I looked down from the plane as it winged its way over deserted dunes and marshes. Lonely, isolated farms on high ground opened a beautiful vista of fertile valleys. But the gentle slopes quietly gave way to formidable mountains whose peaks were partly hidden by fluffy white clouds. Somehow the invisible is always more fascinating than stark reality; it seems to hold those secrets for which men have died through the ages.

The merging colors, reminiscent of a Japanese rice painting, displaced the most recent scenes of fashionable hotels along the bay of Acapulco. Gone were the tall modern buildings, the glaring neon signs, and the noisy motors of our mechanized twentieth century. The harmonious landscape unfolding below was timeless, simple, and soothing to the senses.

Only minutes away from my destination, there was no city in sight and even after we landed at the small airfield, there was no sign of Oaxaca, the capital of the state by the same name. The half-hour drive by cab leads through

57

peaceful country whose people, passing unhurriedly along the road, seem to reflect the calmness which marks the whole region from the mellow green of the fields to the spotless white worn by the men and the starched skirts and embroidered blouses of the women.

Oaxaca, at the foot of the wild peaks of the Sierras, was built by the Spaniards on the site of the ancient Indian capital. Legend has it that a race of giants first ruled the storied hills where crumbling ruins of temples and tombs now only whisper tales of the ancient culture which once flourished there. But the dark-eyed descendants of the Zapotec and Mixtec Indians who pass you on the street in their traditional costumes are as real as the impressive churches or the pillared arcades which shelter stores and outdoor venders around the main square.

Although the church of Santo Domingo, a superb example of early Baroque, founded by the Dominicans in the sixteenth century, is by far more impressive than the shrine of the Virgin of La Soledad, it is there, on the spot where the Virgin is said to have appeared, that Oaxacans gather every December 18th to pay homage to their patron saint in a fiesta which is unsurpassed in richness.

Like most tourists who come to Oaxaca, I soon headed for Monte Alban, Mexico's holy mountain. Centuries ago Zapotec Indians built a whole religious city there at the junction of three valleys. On this island rising a thousand feet from the green sea of fertility below, Zapotec architects had leveled the hilltop to build a two-mile-long city of tombs and temples.

On two huge rectangular courts, raised pyramidal altars and shrines decorated with monumental friezes of intricate sculpture are accessible in the center by great flights of stairs which alternate with smooth slopes of masonry to wall in the entire courts. A treasure of jewels, goblets, earrings, and armlets chiseled out of jade, turquoise, and gold has been found in one of the tombs belonging to a Mixtecan nobleman. Occasionally, as one wanders through the remains of this ancient city, built to exalt man into communion with divinity, one can hear the eerie notes of a primitive flute accompanied by the tom-tom of a crude drum, but time has not really slipped back as it may seem. Modern descendants, practicing for a church fiesta, create this illusion in a setting which does not need much stimulation to recreate the past.

At the base of Monte Alban lies the serenely peaceful village of Xoxo, whose people seldom make concessions to modern life or to new ideas which would change their customary way of living. Nothing seems to disturb these people. Guadelupe Lopez, born there in one of the small adobe houses, was no exception. He had led an uneventful life until he was almost thirty. He had remained faithful to the customs and traditions of his Zapotec tribe and tended his father's field with the same primitive tools his ancestors had used many generations before him. Yet, he knew more about the mysterious cycle of plant life than many farmers trained in modern agricultural schools. He revered and respected nature and recognized the forces which had sustained him and his fields.

When an *espanto,* or evil spirit, struck Jose, Guadelupe's younger brother, he turned overnight into a frightened and possessed creature. Neither the expensive patent medicine ordered from a mail-order house in Mexico City, nor the prayers of the Catholic priest brought any relief as Jose went from bad to worse. Normally of good appetite, he now had difficulties in swallowing and the slightest noise frightened him so much that he could not be left alone for a moment. He began to hear voices everywhere and saw in Pinto, their old dog, a vicious jaguar. Even the glorious skyline of their sacred mountain turned suddenly into an image of Cocijo, the God of the Rain.

The Catholic priest, ordinarily a gentle and most patient man almost lost his temper when he heard the ominous word *espanto*. It made him aware how little progress his Church had made since Spanish missionaries had converted Jose's ancestors more than three centuries ago. When he surprised some of his people practicing their ancient rituals right after he had finished his own brief Sunday service, he sometimes wondered where he had failed, but his superior kept on reassuring him that it takes a long time to destroy the superstitious belief of the people.

At times Jose would break into a heated argument with himself or with people he imagined to be present. Calm nerves, the one and only gift Zapotecs hand down to their people, had been taken from Jose by evil spirits his brother thought as he followed his monologue which at first made no sense at all. Yet, as he listened more closely, it became clear that Jose was talking about some intruders who had attempted to defile the sacred mountain.

As Guadelupe listened to his brother's ravings, he began to wonder if Jose had taken it upon himself to become the instrument of the gods' revenge. Thanks to his infinite patience, he soon came to the conclusion that his brother had participated in an attack on a team of archeologists who had come to Oaxaca to start excavation on the holy resting places in search of a lost city.

Though the Mexican government made an attempt to discover who ambushed these scientists, not the slightest trace of evidence was ever uncovered, and the people's lips remained sealed. But if Jose was permitted to go on with his self-induced frenzy, it would be only a matter of days before his identity became known. Shielding him from the law would be difficult, Guadelupe figured correctly, but even assuming that it could be done, how much longer could he endure the physical strain which sapped the last drop of strength out of his system? Looking at his suffering brother, shivering under a heavy sarape in spite of the stifling heat, his mind was made up.

The *benihucuagua,* an ancient seer, lived in an isolated cave at the outskirts of the village. On rare occasions when he came to the market, people avoided him and mothers called their children indoors. His weatherbeaten features defied any guess of his age, and he did not seem to mind the distance people kept from him. After all, it was a common knowledge that all villagers not only provided for his livelihood, but that they, and many from far away places, came to see him whenever they were in need of help.

Quietly the two brothers walked through the empty village as a hungry hawk circled overhead defying the twilight and the sanctity of the approaching night. Like two silhouettes they moved through the early night till their trained eyes saw a faint flicker in the distance marking their destination.

The old man sat near the entrance of his dwelling which was part shack, part cave. A slight nod of his head was the only welcome he extended. As Jose followed the old man into the cave, Guadelupe, waiting outside, fed dry twigs to the small fire.

The *benihucuagua* or *brucho*, as they are sometimes called, led Jose to an oddly shaped block of wood and motioned him to sit down. A pleasant, faintly spicy odor filled the air as the *brucho* began to wave a branch of soft leaves rhythmically in front of Jose's face. His penetrating, deep-set eyes soon found and held those of his ward who, under the spell of this ancient ritualistic tranquilizer, began to calm down and to relate how his sleep had turned into a torture.

When Jose finally stopped talking the *brucho* reached for an earthenware container and a loud and distinct voice called Jose's name into the narrow opening. Then he placed the bottle to Jose's ear so he could hear the echo coming from the hollow jar. Reciting some ancient phrases in the tradition of the Zapotecs, he declared the evil spirit captured and ordered Jose's soul to return as undisturbed as it had been before. Then he tapped Jose gently on the shoulder allowing him to awaken gradually from his deep trance.

It was past midnight when the two brothers returned to their village. Tired, but no longer afraid of the dark, Jose greeted his old parents who had stayed up to pray for his recovery. To whom they prayed remains as much a secret as the *brucho's* method and power to break the spell of the *espanto*.

Jose's nightmare is no product of the imagination but a real case history. One of Mexico's best-known historians and anthropologists explained to me that nearly all messages received from the supernatural come through the medium of dreams or visions to those who possess the ability to read and interpret them. These visions can be gained by extreme privations, by purifying the vision through hunger, or by the use of drugs.

To induce ecstatic conditions, the Indians made use of many different methods that ranged from want of sleep, seclusion, pertinacious fixing of the mind upon a certain subject, to the swallowing or inhalation of cerebral intoxicants such as maguey, coca, or the peyotl. In olden days visions were also induced by winding the skin of a freshly killed animal around the neck until the pressure on the veins produced unconsciousness. The resulting dreams were often caused by a possible overflow of blood to the head.

The intoxicant peyotl lasts for several days and induces trance. It comes from a specie of the vinagrilla, having a white tuberous root which is the part used for this drug. This root is masticated and then placed into a wooden mortar for fermentation. Another drug for the purpose of inducing ecstatic visions was an unguent known as teopatli, a compound of seeds of various plants, the ashes of spiders, scorpions, and other poisonous insects.

The *brucho*, also known as *naualli*, is usually quite adept in astrology. He times his magical sessions either during the second, fifth, or seventh hour of the night which are most dreaded by common people because they are presided over by gods of evil repute and thus are considered more favorable to the appearance of demons.

The people of Xoxo consider themselves the traditional guardians of the holy mountain and they still resent the intrusion of outsiders not in tune with their own spiritual insight.

THE SOLDIER PROPHET

Jane Allen

In times of stress, prophets are taken out of their winding sheets and for the duration of the emergency the light of their forecast shines anew. The resurrection occasions a marveled flurry of interest, and when the crisis passes the prophet is cavalierly re-interred and his voice once again stilled.

So it happened for Homer Lea, American prophet without honor in his own country, who was disinterred in March of 1942 by Clare Boothe Luce via the *Saturday Evening Post.*

This brief resurrection was occasioned by the fact that in 1909, thirty-two years before the attack on Pearl Harbor, in his book *The Valor of Ignorance,* Lea thundered a solemn warning that the Japanese were resolutely and methodically preparing for such an attack:

"Japan's future depends upon secure and widely distributed naval bases so strategically placed that they give her command over all routes of trade in the Pacific . . ."

At the time Lea wrote, Japan had eliminated China from the Pacific; and with the assistance of England, had crushed Russia in the same ocean. Future expansion demanded that she get control of those bastions in the Pacific administered by the United States.

And Japan, Lea noted bitterly, was quite fortunate. The United States in "the valor of her ignorance" was unprepared.

"The republic, [America] drunk with the vanity of its potential resources, will not differentiate between them and actual power. Japan, with infinitely less resources, is militarily forty times more powerful . . . A nation can become so rich that its very wealth will bankrupt it in a war with a country poor and frugal and warlike . . . All the riches of the world cannot supply national unity nor that perseverance which is unappalled by disaster . . ."

Like Job of old, Lea cried his warning.

He even prepared a blueprint of just how Japan would attack at Linguyen and quite easily take the Philippines, this before the emphasis on air power.

Lea followed with another book, *Day of the Saxon,* in which he foretold the inevitable aggression of Germany against England, for Germany could not expand her sphere of interests without encroaching on the British Empire. Nor could she hope to accomplish her purpose except "by the invasion and investment of the British Isles themselves . . ."

At the same time he said Germany could not hazard any adventure in Russia. "A war between Russia and Germany, while resulting disastrously to the defeated nation, will in the end bring no gains to the victor commensurate with its expenditure . . . But the dismemberment of the British Empire, on the other hand, will result most advantageously to Germany, Russia, and Japan."

For dismemberment of the British Empire would give both Russia and Japan the opportunity to snatch India, as India was the key to the Empire and to Asiatic power.

England, Lea warned, was so concerned over Germany's ambitions she gave scant heed to Russia, which since the early eighteenth century "has moved onward with elemental propulsion" and by waging twenty-one wars in two centuries had expaned her dominion from less than two hundred and seventy-five thousand square miles to nearly nine million, or one-seventh of the land surface of the world.

Actually, he wrote, Germany, Russia, and Japan could co-exist very nicely, dividing the world between them. To Japan would go the Pacific and its islands; to Russia the Southern Asian continent and the Indian Ocean; to Germany that of Western and Southern Europe, the Mediterranean, and the Atlantic.

Should America be victorious in the unavoidable conflict with Japan, and England survive the thrust from Germany, England would be so debilitated that America would automatically inherit her mantle of power. In that eventuality, with Germany and Japan presumably defeated, America as the leading world power would face the third aggressor, Russia. Lea was working on this premise in *The Day of the Slav* when he died in 1912.

And these atmospheric convulsions, prophesied Lea, would happen regardless of what governments were in power at the time of their aggression which, considering the tide of events since Lea wrote his books, should give pause for thought to those shrill voices screaming of Communism and Fascism.

Clare Boothe Luce first heard of Homer Lea shortly

before that dark day of December 7, 1941, from a Colonel Charles Willoughby who believed that Lea's prediction about Japan would soon be a grim actuality, as indeed it was.

Was Lea, queried Miss Boothe, some sort of Nostradamus?

"Homer Lea," stated Colonel Willoughby, "was neither mystic nor prophet. He was a scientist. He studied the science of war—the fundamental laws of which are immutable as those of any other science."

And with that summation, this writer could hardly agree less. Certainly Lea was a student of the science of war, but most assuredly he was a prophet. Prophecy is prediction, and prediction is arrived at variously.

There is religious prophecy based on revelation; prediction by palmistry and fortune telling. Clairvoyance is based in antiquity on unverifiable laws. But there is also deductive predictability, based on verifiable laws, and this could be termed creative prophecy. Certainly, Homer Lea, without peer in his specialized field, was a creative and true prophet.

He was as much mystic as Joan of Arc, for a series of strange prophetic dreams he had as a child compelled him to an historic adventure even more unique in its way than the saga of the Maid who heard voices that summoned her to the aid of France.

Homer Lea, American, a frail hunchback since birth, a scant five feet tall, was to become a three-star General in the Chinese war for independence against the Manchu dowager empress, Tzu-Hei!

Homer was born in 1876, the son of Alfred Lea, who was no mean stalwart himself, having at the age of sixteen made his way alone through war-torn Kansas in a mule-drawn covered wagon to the Rockies. Alfred Lea settled in Cripple Creek, Colorado, married, fathered Homer and his two sisters, and in 1892, when Homer was sixteen, moved his family to Los Angeles.

Homer never grew beyond his twelfth year and his schoolmates called him Little Scrunch-Neck. From his earliest years, Little Scrunch-Neck was determined, in spite of his deformity and frailty, to become a soldier. Soldiering was the only game he played, drilling his schoolmates after school and at home playing at war games with his two sisters. July the Fourth was not a day to set off firecrackers. It was a day for war games, the firecrackers serving as artillery pieces to blast his sisters from untenable positions.

Why his sisters and schoolmates meekly took orders from the sickly little hunchback, they never could explain. But a Chinese who was with him on the field of battle said years later, "He had eyes that could bury you nine feet under the ground if you disobeyed him."

A schoolmate said that Lea's militarism and interest in all things Chinese stemmed from the family cook, a pigtailed Chinaman who fired the boy's imagination with bloodthirsty tales of Chinese wars.

But the late Harry Carr, of the *Los Angeles Times,* said Homer confided to him that as a child he had a series of prophetic dreams in which he saw himself revealed as the reincarnation of an historic Chinese warrior called the Martial Monk, marching at the head of his army to defend China.

Homer was, understandably, considered somewhat eccentric by his teachers, but there was nothing eccentric about his scholastic record. He averaged over ninety in Latin, Greek, French, history, and mathematics.

In 1894, he entered Occidental College, majoring in classical languages and history, but his primary extracurricular activity was military matters. Now instead of playing war games with broomsticks and firecrackers, he expostulated about the campaigns of Caesar, Hannibal, Alexander, and Napoleon. And he learned Chinese.

Though Lea entered Stanford in 1895 to study law, his main interest was military, with a particular emphasis on the Chinese. At this time there was considerable focus on China and the Empress Tzu-Hei. The original Dragon Lady of the comic strips, she sat on China's Dragon Throne weaving unladylike and bloodthirsty plots against her enemies.

Lea was a gifted orator, and in his rich low voice he expounded on what he called "the hemispheric wars between nations." On his walls were huge maps, and with colored pins he waged wars between the Japanese and Germans on one side, and China and the United States on the other. Or sometimes the war would be between Russia and Great Britain with India as the prize.

Not unnaturally Lea believed in the status quo, the Saxon world, as he called it, dominated by Britain and the United States, and he was sorely troubled that the people of these two powers were fattening upon their prosperity and blind to the expanding predatory powers waiting to pounce.

"A nation which is rich, vain, and at the same time unprepared, provokes wars and hastens its ruin . . ."

He flailed politicians, pacifists, the clericalists, isolationists, and, of all things, had hard words to say about the feminists.

England and America must, he exhorted, stand firm and together always, and a free China would be America's natural ally against Russia and Japan.

He now practiced a bit of isolationism himself, consorting almost exclusively with Chinese students and spending weekends in San Francisco's Chinatown where he came in contact with members of the Po-Wong Wui, a secret society of intellectual young Chinese dedicated to waging civil war against the armies of the Dragon Lady.

His military preoccupation earned the bitter and undying enmity of Dr. Jordan, President of Stanford University, an avowed pacifist who found Lea "vulgar, loud-mouthed, excessively warlike . . ." In fact, two years before the outbreak of the first World War which Lea predicted, Doctor Jordan published a paper in which he called Lea an "ambitious romancer, a crippled dwarf," and *The Valor of Ignorance* "mischievous, worthless, and nonsense."

The Spanish American War of 1898 was a period of awful frustration for the young warrior. His schoolmates enlisted but all Lea could do was join a college cavalry troop consisting of, Lea said bitterly, "the lame, the halt, and the blind." In fact, Lea was all three, as an old eye ailment returned to plague him, and in the hospital for treatment he contracted smallpox.

By the time Lea recovered, the war was over, but not for him. To Harry Carr he confided "All great careers are carved out by the sword. Mine, too, I shall carve that way."

70

And when Carr gently reminded him of his physical handicap, Lea rebutted that Lord Byron's club foot had not deterred him in Greece.

"China," he told Carr, "shall be my Greece."

When a schoolmate cautioned him that in China he stood to literally lose his head, Little Scrunch Neck retorted, "They'll have a hard time finding my neck!"

His sisters tried in vain to dissuade him from the Chinese adventure, while his father, in the classic manner, simply cut off his generous allowance. But Lea was not to be intimidated or deterred. He secured backing from the China Reform Association and announced he was being sent as a "secret military agent."

After a rash of publicity in the San Francisco papers, presumably planted by Lea himself, the "secret agent" took off for China.

"I go," he said coolly, "to topple the Manchus from their ancient Dragon Throne."

On his way to China, Lea passed through Hawaii, Guam, and the Philippines, and what he saw and examined along the route gave him his predictive blueprint for *The Valor of Ignorance*, the path for Japanese aggression.

According to Lea's own account he travelled from Canton by palanquin over hundreds of miles, and arrived at Peking unchallenged. Here, agents of the Po-Wong-Wui gave him a letter to the Dragon Lady's own Prime Minister, Kong Yu Wei, who under the very nose of the dowager empress was working to raise a volunteer army with which to overthrow her and place her liberal nephew, Kwang Hsu, on the throne.

Certain factions within the Manchu court held the belief that if the throne could be Occidentalized and China opened up to Western development, China's old prosperity and greatness would be restored. The wicked empress, on the other hand, detested and feared "the white devils" and all their industrial magic which would put an end to her long and brutal reign.

In the Forbidden Palace itself, Lea held a prearranged rendezvous with the Prime Minister, who was not a little startled to see this crippled small foreigner.

"I have come," Lea announced in his inimitable way, "to help you save China from the old tigress. To rescue Kwang Hsu. (Kwang Hsu had been imprisoned by the empress.) To lead your armies to victory."

The prime minister smiled.

"You are very young to do all that."

Lea retorted, "I am the same age Napoleon was at Rivoli."

The prime minister found this audacity amusing, but as the audience continued, he was impressed.

In the end, Lea reported, he was given the Star of the Order of Emperor Kwang Hsu and a commission as lieutenant general in the Army of the Emperor with orders to proceed to Shensi province in north central China and there take over command of a body of volunteers.

This venture was doomed before it began. Within a hundred miles of his destination a runner brought the dire news to Lea that the empress, apprised of the plot, had ordered all of the Prime Minister's sympathizers beheaded. The Prime Minister, himself, warned in time, had fled with a price on his head, and there was a price of $10,000 on the "white devil" Homer Lea.

Officers of the Shensi army were captured and a row of

their heads already decorated the city walls. Thus the Dragon Lady ignited the spark that would start the ghastly episode of the Boxer Rebellion whereby the troops loyal to the Manchu throne swore to rid China of all white men.

Undaunted, Lea sent a runner to the volunteers in Shensi with a message advising retreat to the mountains, and himself calmly set about joining them.

When Lea reached the volunteers, he rallied the broken morale. For months he trained the raw recruits and then, feeling they were ready, marched at their head to Peking.

By the time he arrived outside the gates of the city, the Boxer Rebellion had reached its monstrous climax. The legations and compounds of the white powers, with their women and children, were under siege and in desperate circumstances.

Troops of several powers were fighting to rescue their nationals. General Lea and his troops fought beside the Americans under General Chaffee, and when at long last General Chaffee marched into the walled city, the besieged defenders were confounded to see a midget white man, garbed as a Chinese general, at the head of thousands of ragged troops.

The evil empress fled with her court and the imperial guard. Lea and his raffish army pursued her, but they were waylaid by the imperial guard and routed. Abandoned, Lea took refuge in a Buddhist temple.

It was one of his favorite stories when he returned to America and attended patriotic Chinese rallies, to tell of how a monk dressed a wound in his arm and fed and gave him drink. When Lea reached for a cup, the old monk said, "It is a small hand, but it is a great hand. You will yet lead armies and vanquish your enemies." And as the monk spoke, a small bird dropped from a tree outside, dead. In China there was a superstition that when a bird dropped dead from a tree a great throne would fall.

Lea now escaped to Hong Kong where he took refuge with a Chinese chum from Stanford, a member of the fanatically dedicated Po-Wong-Wui, who meant not only to topple the Dragon Throne but also to establish a Republic in China. And it was here he first met Sun Yat-sen, head of the society, later to be known as the George Washington of China.

Lea was twenty-four at that historic meeting which Sun Yat-sen recorded in his autobiography. The Chinese leader promised Lea that if the revolution succeeded he would make him his chief military adviser.

"Make me that now," the young warrior said, "and you *will* succeed."

Lea returned to San Francisco wearing the sumptuous uniform of a Chinese general which his old friends found as embarrassing as what they considered were tall tales of his Chinese adventures. But when Lea's home became the official headquarters for Doctor Sun and the revolutionary movement and was frequented by Chinese of consequence and standing, the social weather changed to awe. To the press, Doctor Sun and his adherents always referred to Lea as "The General."

General Lea sounded the call for a volunteer army, and with the assistance of Ansel O'Banion, a tough Irish ex-sergeant, trained his troops in the science of modern warfare, drilling them on the outskirts of San Francisco and in the canyons of Santa Monica. Little Scrunch-Neck

74

had come a long way since the warfare games of his child-hood.

He also lectured and organized public rallies where he harangued the crowd, sitting astride O'Banion's broad shoulders. At one such rally so impassioned was his plea to the pigtailed Chinese audience, that in the end they whipped out their pocket knives, and to a man cut off their queues, the symbol of servitude to the Manchus!

But Lea's health, never robust, was failing, and now he was forced to take up the pen instead of the sword. A tour of the unprotected west coast shocked him into writing *The Valor of Ignorance,* his cry to America to prepare for what he considered the inevitable aggression by Japan.

At this time, he was a familiar figure sitting in West-lake Park, a campaign hat on his head, a military cloak lined in red about his shoulders, making his notes of the coming doom.

Later, as his eyes failed, he dictated his notes to his devoted secretary, Mrs. Powers, a widow he subsequently married.

The publication of *The Valor of Ignorance* in 1909 was hailed by General Chaffee and a few other American officers, sold a respectable eighteen thousand copies, created a minor furor, and was denounced by pacifist groups, among them Lea's old enemy David Starr Jordan.

In these days he might be called hard names, too, like fascist, reactionary, etc. But they would be clouded misnomers. Lea was simply a militarist; a chauvinist believing in the status quo of the Anglo-Saxon world. Mainly he was an ardent patriot, perhaps guilty of making overstatement in an effort to arouse his countrymen who were "slothful with fat pride." But let all his detractors remember what Admiral Yamamoto said in December of 1941, "I am looking forward to dictating peace to the United States in the White House at Washington."

The late Randolph Hearst seized upon the book to fatten his circulation. The Hearst press had a field day screaming "Yellow Peril" at its readers, and implying the Japanese would attack at any moment. Time passed without incident, however, and the furor subsided.

The Valor of Ignorance went out of print in 1922, just at the time Japan was fortifying the islands around Wake and Guam which she got from Germany in the Versailles Treaty.

Twenty-four editions of the book sold in Japan and the jacket blurb read, "Excellent reading matter for all Oriental men with red blood in their veins." It was made required reading for officers, and both German and Russian military schools followed suit.

Perhaps the most significant backwash of the book was that an odd twenty years later a certain Adolph Hitler acquired a copy, scribbled notes from it about the indolent way of democracies and incorporated them in a book called *Mein Kampf*. But even Hitler didn't do his studying well, for he ignored Lea's warning that a German attack on Russia would be both futile and disastrous.

Recognition came from both England and Germany. Lord Roberts sent an urgent invitation to Lea, even offering the services of his own physician to accompany him. Kaiser Wilhem II was equally urgent in his request that Lea visit Germany. Perhaps the militant Kaiser, with a withered arm, had a special respect for the little man with a crooked back.

76

But neither Washington nor, more importantly, West Point paid Lea any honor, which is rather a pity, for this above all he wanted.

In 1910, in spite of his growing infirmity, Lea sailed for Europe in the company of Mrs. Powers, now his wife, and his old friend the ex-Prime Minister, Kong Yu Wei.

In full-dress military uniform of his own design, Lea witnessed German maneuvers. The Germans pressed honors upon him which did not swerve Lea from his objectivity in *The Day of the Saxon*. Germany, in her drive for power, he wrote, must of necessity destroy the British Empire to gain her ends. With this Herr Hitler concurred in *Mein Kampf*. He was not afraid of America. Britain was his quarry. Unfortunately for him, he was sidetracked into the Russian venture.

In London, Lea started his notes on the third book, *The Day of the Slav*, which he was never to finish. There Lea received word from his Chinese agents that the long-awaited day had arrived. The revolutionary army of China was ready to strike.

Sun Yat-sen joined Lea in London, and against the entreaties of his physicians, Lea sailed for China with Doctor Sun.

Borne in a palanquin, Little Scrunch-Neck fulfilled that strange series of dreams he had as a boy. He led the victorious army of revolution and made good his promise to topple the Manchus from their Dragon Throne.

Sun Yat-sen was elected President of the Chinese Republic and General Homer Lea was the only white man present at the birth of the new democracy.

In an address he reputedly made to the assembly he

said, "Your republic, like ours, can only be preserved in its beauties and freedom by vigilant swords."

The republic he worked to bring into being is no longer a republic and the alliance he proposed with America a vain conceit. For China is now one of the predatory powers of which he warned. Her break with Russia was not simply the ideological split claimed but the same old contest for power. "For when the sphere of their interests converge, nations go to war." Russia and China are both grappling for control of Southeast Asia with India as the focal point.

Recently, a despatch came from New Delhi that a Tibetan monk who fled to Napal reported the Communist Chinese have massed troops along the Himalayan borders poised for what they termed "the liberation of Asia."

Peking, the monk reported, has circulated literature stating, "India is nothing but a paper tiger. First of all it is our plan to conquer India so we can get all the materials we need for our military to further our Asian plans . . ."

And it would unsettle Lea even further that the feminism he abhorred is on the rise in China.

His dreams realized for the moment, Lea's frail strength collapsed. In Nanking he suffered a stroke that paralyzed his left side. He was carried aboard the boat for America on a litter.

Little Scrunch-Neck came home in May of 1912 and died in November in his Santa Monica cottage. He was buried in his grand uniform, a sword at his side.

THE SPIRIT WORLD TALKS BACK

Dee Hill

I had known Mabel Walrath Smith about six months when she called last August to wish me a happy birthday. Mabel is a well known astrologer, but I had never heard of her until one day at a press club luncheon.

Jane Lait, a prominent Hollywood writer, was remarking how astounding it was to be guided by an astrology chart. I had heard a lot about astrology in the past but I had never given it much thought. As Jane talked I became more interested when she said Mabel had predicted President Kennedy's assassination and also the Alaskan earthquake months before these events took place. Even though I didn't believe in astrology, that sounded like good story material to me so I asked Jane to introduce Mabel to a nonbeliever.

After that introduction, my life has never been quite the same. I not only got a good story, but I got my first personal astrology chart and contacted the spirit world too. But, I'm getting way ahead of myself; contacting the spirit world came months after the first interview.

While I watched Mabel draw up my chart I realized

that it wasn't fortune telling mumbo-jumbo but a definite mathematical science. Chaldean astrology has been around since before Christ, but it is the most difficult planet probing to master. Mabel Smith is the oldest known living Chaldean astrologer. She was eighty three years old last August 8, 1964. "I'll never live to see my 90th birthday," she says with certainty, "I've beaten the stars seven times, the eighth time will get me. I'll choke to death in my sleep. When my aspects are bad, I don't sleep."

When she handed me my chart, I noticed a lot of what she wrote down about me was very close to my nature. It was interesting and fun reading. I thanked her but she could sense I was still a skeptic. She had predicted that my feet would lead me to my death. That I should watch where I walk and take very good care of my lower extremities.

One day I walked into the office of a friend who hadn't seen me in months, and he jumped up exuberantly, grabbed me around the waist and swung me to the side in a humorous gesture of friendliness. Suddenly I felt a stabbing pain in my left toe. My left foot had slammed into a bookcase so hard that as soon as I took my shoe off the toe began to swell.

Immediately Mabel's prediction came to my mind. I had never had anything happen to my feet before in my life. They had always been in excellent condition, and even doctors had remarked that the pointed toe shoe, which has increased foot trouble 79 per cent, hadn't marred my foot at all. However, after that night I wound up at the chiropodist's office with a sprained toe that needed treatment in a hurry.

Shortly after that incident, Mabel called to wish me a happy birthday and to invite me and my husband out to dinner. When I told her I'd be limping a little because of a slight toe injury she wasn't a bit surprised. She was sorry but she had warned me it was in my chart.

During dinner she told me a strange tale of a rather unbelievable phenomenon.

"Now," she said in a secretive tone, "I'm going to tell you something that is very confidential. I want you to break this story to the world Dee, but I can't tell you the names of the people involved until we get their okay."

Then she began, "Twenty-nine years ago I was at a small dinner party at a friend's house with my husband. After dinner they started playing games and the hostess took out a Ouija board. They asked me to join in but I said no, I'd rather watch. Then someone put the Ouija board on my lap and I immediately felt sleepy. I said, 'Take this thing off my lap and let me rest for just five minutes.' I had hardly finished the sentence when I fell asleep right in front of a dozen people.

"They said my head slumped to the side in a sort of deep slumber but my middle finger started pointing to letters on the board. Someone had a pencil and paper and they started taking down the letters until they formed words. When a word was formed my hand would come to the top of the board and then begin again. A girl's name came on the board and identified herself as the spiritual guide of someone in the room but she said she could not be his guide much longer and she went on to predict her own rebirth.

"She gave the name that she would have on earth, where and when she would be born and who her parents would be." Mabel took a deep breath. "That girl is now twenty-five years old. I have gone to the place she predicted she would be born and made a photostat copy of her birth certificate. Everything checked out and now I have the proof. This could make the whole world believe in the hereafter if I can only get her father's permission to tell the girl and the world. But it must be handled delicately. Perhaps it would be too much of a shock to the girl. Perhaps the family would rather not have the notoriety."

All this time my husband, Irwin Zucker, who is by career a publicity man, and I had been sitting quietly, intrigued by the fascinating story. Irwin said, "Mabel, if you wanted to, you could start a night-club act and tour the country just telling people about themselves from their astrology charts. At eighty-three you'd be a sensation."

Mabel smiled, "I'll give it some thought." And you could tell even at eighty-three she was considering the idea seriously.

"Mabel," I said, "I'd like to go on the board with you. Maybe a spirit guide will talk to me." I said it almost "tongue in cheek" and she could tell it was a challenge.

"It tires me so," she said, giving it some consideration, "but I, too, would like to find out if you have a spirit guide. Yes, I'll come over to your house tomorrow and we'll go on the board."

It was settled. The next day I picked her up and took her back to my house. Then I sent the twins to the park with the maid so that we could have complete quiet.

Mabel sat in a comfortable overstuffed front room chair and I sat opposite her in a straight backed kitchen chair

82

with a pad and pencil in my hands. I placed the board in Mabel's lap and she made some small talk which got me rather impatient with the whole scene.

"I can't force the sleep," she explained, "it'll come. I'm starting to feel sleepy now."

Suddenly her eyes closed and absolutely nothing happened for about one minute. I smiled to myself, took a deep breath, and was about to put the pad and pencil down when her middle finger started to move across the board pointing to different letters.

This is what I took down. "Dee, this is your guide. I was a singer. I was called Melba. I was named after a city in Australia, Melbourne. One of your twins should be trained as a singer. It is the twin that comes from your body first."

Just about then I glanced at Mabel to see if she was still sleeping. Her eyes were closed, her head was a little to the side and saliva was dripping out of the corner of her mouth. A car went by outside and her muscles jumped as if to awaken her. All this time her finger had been moving but I wasn't taking down anything. I was much too astonished. Then she moaned a little sigh and I started taking down the words again.

"Dee, I have been in this room since you entered the house. I am always with you."

I couldn't believe it. I threw the pad and pencil in the air and gently shook Mabel awake. She blinked, "What happened?"

I said, "Why did you tell me to train one of my twins as a singer?"

She said, "I give up. Why did I tell you to train one of your twins as a singer?"

I shook my head, "Mabel this is what came on the board. I missed quite a bit but I found out who my spiritual guide is."

Mabel looked at the pad. "Melba a singer?" She frowned, "It seems to me I remember a famous opera singer named Melba. She was well-known when I was a teenager. Why don't we go to the library and look her up.

"Good idea," I said jumping up. I still had my doubts as to finding a singer named Melba in the library. But we walked around the corner to the Studio City Branch and asked the librarian where we would find a singer named Melba who might have been well-known 50 years ago. The librarian nodded, went to a shelf and pulled out the thick *Encyclopedia of Musicians*. She thumbed through it then handed the book over opened to a page with the picture of a sweet kind-faced woman. "This is the only Melba in the book," she said.

"Thank you," I nodded, taking the book from her. "Mabel take a look," I said flabbergasted, "her real name was Helen Porter Mitchell. She was born May 19, 1859 and she died February 23, 1931 at the age of seventy-two. In 1886 she took the stage name of Melba and was often referred to as Dame Nellie Melba. She had one of the most outstanding voices in opera."

Mabel was just as excited as I was at finding the information and we both read a short summary of her life.

"This is spooky," I shivered, "and incredible. If I didn't see it with my own eyes I wouldn't believe it. And I'm not even sure if I do now. I'd like to see these spirits."

Then it was Mabel's turn to shiver. "Not me. Don't ask me to help them materialize. Just hearing from them is enough for me. I don't want to see them."

I laughed. "You sound like you're afraid."

She shrugged, "Everybody has their idiosyncrasies and that's mine. Once when I heard a lot of rattling and cracking of the wood in my room I sensed the spirits were around and I prayed they would go away and leave me alone."

"Well," I said, "I would love to see them. I'm sure they wouldn't come around to hurt us as the Hollywood horror films would have you believe. I always like to see who I'm talking to."

"You really are a Doubting Thomas," Mabel smiled.

"No doubt about that. Mabel, I'd like to go on that darn Ouija board again. Only next time I'll try to take down everything your finger points to. Sometimes your hand was going so fast I wasn't sure what you were pointing to and other times it went so slow I guessed the word before it was finished."

Mabel promised we'd go on the board again in a few days and I could hardly wait.

The next night at 10 P.M., I was sitting opposite Mabel in her front room. The Ouija board was on her lap, and I had plenty of white paper and three pencils ready. This is what came on the board.

"This is your Melba friend. It is better that you not have water on the grounds of your house. One of your children can be hurt, and it is the child that came first from your body of the twins. You must sell your house before the New Year. If you do not there will be a near death accident to your oldest child on the bicycle. Your book will be made into a movie. There will be much interest in it in November. The black and white war in the world is working up to a war around the world. It will

85

not start until December 1972. This will start a World War all over in August 1973. This war lasts five years. Rest now. I will talk to you again soon."

Slowly Mabel opened her eyes. She looked very happy and yet a bit sadly wistful.

"I saw such a beautiful kind face." Mabel said. "She was smiling at me. She thanked me for spelling her words." Then tears ran down Mabel's cheeks and I too felt sadly wistful.

"Who would believe me?" I said, "It doesn't matter; it's one of the most thrilling experiences I have ever had and that's good enough for me."

Mabel nodded, "For many things there is no logical explanation."

There may be no logical explanation yet, but I, personally, can hardly wait to return to that Borderline world soon again.

NEW DIRECTIONS IN ASTROLOGY?

Dane Rudhyar

It is now a little more than one century since the last person officially taught astrology in a university of the German Rhineland. There have been recent attempts in Holland to have astrology incorporated in what we would call an extension department course in a university; and in Lille, France, a short-lived *Academie Nationale d'Astrologie* was formed in 1947 which held its opening meetings in the University, mostly because the founder of the Academy, Paul Dupas, was also working at the university in an important administrative function.

Occasionally, in America, astrology enters a campus by some side door, as when I lectured on astrology at the Colorado Springs University in 1946. I was invited to do so by a German professor whose class was studying Schiller's tragedy *Wallenstein*. A good deal of astrology is mentioned throughout several scenes of the play and the students wanted to know what the references meant.

Since that last academic course on astrology ended in our Western world a century ago, much has happened in the field of this ancient method of enquiry into the meaning and the rhythm of unfolding of human experience. For a time very little indeed was known about astrology in our Western society, but a slow revival of interest began with the spread of Theosophical literature after 1875. In England, men like Sepharial and Alan Leo, and later Evangeline Adams in New York, succeeded in starting a new wave of interest in astrology.

With the success of Paul Clancy's *American Astrology,* in 1933–34, this wave of interest took on a tidal character in terms of a popularized version of astrology. Sun-sign astrology. Soon many newspapers here, and later in Europe, were carrying daily or weekly forecasts for the twelve signs of the zodiac. For the first time in history people began to say: "I am a Taurus; what are you?" Astrology became an often most profitable large-scale business.

We know from ancient records that a certain type of astrolgly was the very foundation of the old traditional Chinese civilization, that it pervaded every human activity—including the most intimate phase of the conjugal life—in India. It seems likely that our classical European type of astrology came from Chaldea via Asia Minor and Greece. Both the Egyptian and the Mayan cultures featured astrology especially for historical and agricultural purposes.

Astrology has been called "the mother of all sciences" because all sciences are based implicitly on the belief that our universe is a universe of order and law, that events recur whenever their causes are reproduced under controllable circumstances, and that, therefore, predictability is a fact. Such a belief in an ordered universe and in man's capacity to predict what will happen when certain re-

88

quired conditions are satisfied has been the foundation of astrology since the very dawn of human consciousness.

Primitive man living in a jungle state on a planet enveloped at first by constant fog discovered, once he experienced the clear sky, that there was above him a realm of regular, cyclic, and, therefore, predictable occurrences. This sky realm became for him the very image of order, in contrast to the fearsome chaotic darkness of the jungle. He discovered in temperate regions the regular yearly rhythm of the seasons, also the periodical rhythm of high and low water in the rivers, on the banks of which he developed the rudiments of agriculture. The erection of a reliable *calendar* became an imperative necessity of the agricultural, vitalistic, and tribal societies of early days. This was the beginning of astrology.

Later on as tribes grew into large kingdoms, more abstract intellectual thinking developed, the astrology of old which was used only for collective, agricultural, religious, or state purposes came to be applied to the lives of individual persons: first the king and his reign, then important people of the aristocracy, big merchants, etc. In Greece, Alexandria, and Rome this individualistic use of astrology was prominent; and it was carried over to the European Renaissance period and the Classical era. Yet even in Europe—and even more in the near-East—astrology formed the operative base of most alchemical and Kabbalistic procedures. We find it emphasized in the healing arts, particularly by Paracelsus, and in a more mystical, yet alchemico-psychological sense by Jakob Boehme.

Today a great deal of confusion might be avoided if one realized that one should speak of astrolog*ies* rather than of astrology, just as one cannot really speak of modern psychology, for we are confronted with several psychologies, each of which has a definable use and purpose. It is particularly important to speak of astrologies in the plural if one attempts to speculate upon the future of astrology in the decades or centuries ahead of us. Eventually these different types may become somewhat integrated, but if they are, it will probably be because a still more complex—or, who knows! perhaps simpler—type of approach to the experience and the understanding of a still more universal principle of order has become possible.

It would seem necessary at any rate to differentiate two basic types of astrological enquiries. One of them refers to what I have called "ambiant astrology," the other "individual astrology." These two types may not seem so distinct at the present time, though they have become more differentiated of late by the introduction of the sidereal or star time zodiac and by the attitude of those astrologers who foster its use. They should grow much more apart in the future, for while ambiant astrology will tend to become increasingly scientific in its techniques as well as its essential motivation, individual astrology should develop more than ever in depth and in the direction of an art as well as a psychotherapy, or more specifically as a form of guidance to individuals seeking to reach a greater degree of personality integration.

Ambiant astrology is interested in the prognostication of physical-plane events, just as any of the typically modern sciences are. The most characteristic of modern sciences deal with material systems, for instance physics or chemistry. They are predictive techniques, for they state what can be expected to happen under precisely defined conditions. They deal with events which, theoretically at least, can be observed under controlled experimental conditions, i.e., in laboratory. However, when we reach the type of events, the scope and character of which no laboratory can effectively contain, the methods to be used inevitably must change.

Meteorology geophysics, and all the sciences dealing with our planet as a whole, or with the universe, are Borderline sciences in that they are more descriptive and interpretative than experimental. However unfortunate the recent attempts by American scientists to interfere with the electro-magnetic currents surrounding our globe tried to make of our whole planet a laboratory, it is probable that future generations of scientists will attempt even more doubtful experiments, whether in the realm of geophysics and weather control, or that of biology and genetic transformation.

Today we know that the space surrounding the planets is not a void. The whole solar system appears, at least to the scientific mind, as a vast field of forces, and the periodic, regular motion of the planets and of a variety of smaller bodies must obviously generate in such a field powerful currents of induction. We speak already of "solar winds," and no doubt many subtle and as yet unrecognized types of energy currents will gradually be discovered. Space is a plenum, or a fullness, as opposed to a vacuum, and modern science is coming to a conception of it which may not differ too much from the old occult idea of the true "astral world" which was described as the realm of pure forces.

We earth beings live in this world of energies, a world in which material objects now are seen to dissolve into fields of forces structured by an as yet mysterious principle of order. Humanity, as a kingdom of life, appears related to every other kingdom; its life history and the growth and death of civilizations are structured by the rhythm of glacial ages, by the rise and sinking of continents, by droughts on a vast scope and changes in oceanic or stratospheric currents. The planet is our ambiant. We live *in* it—for it extends thousands of miles above its solid surface, perhaps up to the moon. We live in this "sublunar realm" as well as on continents and seas, just as the nervous system of a man operates within his body and an electro-magnetic aura surrounding it. Humanity has its function as an organ of the planet, Earth, just perhaps as the brain has its own function in a human body. It must, therefore, be affected by whatever affects the whole earth —thus *by the state of the solar system as a whole at any moment*. This solar system is our ambiant. We develop *as human beings* in close relationship to it. Modern ecologists tell us that we must understand a person or a race not as an isolated phenomenon, but in its inter-relationship with its environment.

As the environment of mankind is the planet and beyond it the larger whole of the solar system—for we cannot fail to include in our environment the sun, source of all terrestrial energies—to understand man, we must see him in relation to this solar system. This is where ambiant astrology comes in. It is in principle the science of studying the inter-relationship of man and the solar system as a field of energies.

However, if it is to be a science in the modern sense of the term, it must leave by the wayside its ancient traditions, just as chemistry had to forget alchemy in order to be a "true" science. It must deal with energies that are known, with the state of the solar system "in the vicinity of" the Earth. It should fundamentally deal with mankind as a whole for it is, from such a point of view, mankind *as a whole* that is affected by the solar system.

Why should any individual person in Los Angeles, for example, be differently affected by this cosmic ambiant than any other? One may answer: because each person has his own way of reacting to the pressures and the changes in his environment. Granted; but the problem of explaining *how* the individual's reactions depend on the positions of the planets at his birth is a very difficult one. Here we deal with the traditional methods of an astrology which was based upon a philosophy of life entirely different from our own today. Can we accept this philosophy? Can we accept the principle of the "correspondence" of microcosm and macrocosm? If we do we can hardly pretend to be "scientific" in the modern sense of the term. But is it important or necessary that we should appear "scientific"? Could there not be validity in a type of astrology which would be a discipline of thought entirely different from modern science; which would be—as it was in the past—an art, or as it could be, a branch of psychotherapy in association with a new form of depth psychology?

We are haunted by the evident achievements of a science hypnotized by technology. We crave to know the "how to" in every field. Technique dominates our consciousness. But we should realize—and many do today— that the preoccupation with technique is but too often the enemy of understanding. Modern man wants to know how to do a myriad of things without any real understanding of *why* they are worth doing. Thus the preoccupation of a great many astrologers today is to "prove" that astrology is a technique for the prediction of clear-cut events evident to anybody; but very few bother to ask whether such a type of predictive science would have value for man and would increase his understanding of himself and of others. It could prove psychologically destructive in that it could generate fear on a large scale. Still, "events-oriented" astrologers are hard at work using the tools of modern scientific intellect to transform fortune-telling astrology into a statistical science. The unanswered question is, I repeat, whether astrology as a statistical science would not be as opposed to a true understanding of the life of an individual person—indeed as potentially inimical to the development of a person's spiritual integrity—as the usual type of fortune telling has been and is when the client fully trusts and depends upon the "clairvoyant."

The issue, I believe, is clear. There should be two kinds of astrology. One type would deal with human collectivities in the spirit of all the sciences which deal with large-scale events on the planet. This includes sociology, economics, the broader aspects of politics, and the historical evolution of humanity as a whole. It would be a new and much expanded form of the old mundane astrology which modern conditions have made largely obsolete in its methods and its reliance on most questionable traditional concepts. The other type of astrology would be one which deals with individual persons, *not* in terms of predicting what will happen to them, but as a psychological technique aiming at developing an ever greater understanding and a fuller, richer integration of the total

person. This, of course, is what natal astrology is supposed to do even today. But while astrologers talk about
such an aim and some clients assent to the concept,
actually the foremost preoccupation in both the client's
and the astrologer's minds is the prediction of what will
happen. An astrologer is considered remarkably good if
his predictions turn out to be correct.

The essential factor in such an approach must be a
consideration of the *birth chart as a whole* in relation to
the whole life of the whole person. This means a basic
revaluation of most astrological techniques used today.
What counts in such a type of astrology is the entire
process of individual existence which begins at the first
breath, when the fundamental rhythms of the organism
are established; the rhythm of the blood circulation and
that of the breath, to which perhaps a third rhythm will
be added in time, that of the nervous energy along the
spine.

The life of a person is a *process*—the process of actuali-
zation of the potential of existence and consciousness
inherent in the first act of individualization, the first
breath. This process has many phases; and obviously these
phases are related to events. But unless these events are
understood in terms of the whole process of individual
existence—conditioning the phases of this process but
also being conditioned by the basic *needs* of the person—
they have no personal significance.

The one primary purpose of psychology, of psychotherapy, and also of course of all spiritual techniques of
integration is to understand the meaning of events of
one's life and of the multitude of organic and psychic
processes which undertone everyday existence and its

concrete events. But there are different kinds and degrees of understanding. One may think one understands some relatively isolated event and its immediate causes and results. Yet there can be no real and total individuality until the event is seen as an expression of a particular phase of the entire life process and this phase is understood within the frame of reference of this total process.

What the astrology of which I am now speaking can theoretically do (the practice is of course very difficult!) is to make us understand and accept the "structure" of the life process, our destiny, and of the total organism of personality (body and psyche), our individuality. Astrology deals essentially with the structure of processes, or we might say, with *the order inherent in any organized system of activities*. From the astrological point of view such a structural order is inherent in the first act of individuality; one might call this the *logos* of the life cycle, or the "seed" of what will (or should) emerge as a relatively unique full-grown individual person. It is *because* this astrology of the individual person deals with relatively unique wholes of existence that it cannot be a science in the modern sense of the term. Science does *not* deal with individuals but only with statistical groups or large collectivities fitted into specific classes.

When the old astrologer spoke of the equivalence of microcosm and macrocosm, he referred to existential wholes, a universe and a man, or, in earlier times when the concept of the individual person was hardly developed, the planet, Earth. What this equivalence meant was that the *structuring factors* controlling the unfoldment of the microcosm's life processes were analogical to those controlling the cyclic processes of the universe as a whole. This is not, and probably it can never be, a scientifically demonstrable statement. Yet it could be taken as an intuitively perceived postulate, and it would be valid if, *on the basis of it,* a richer and more fulfilling understanding of a person's life could be reached. That it can thus be reached is what seems evident to anyone who has grasped the real meaning of this astrology of the individual person and who uses constructively its tools. It is a use which, alas, poses many problems!

In the strict sense of the term this cannot be, at least today, a scientific approach. But what I have called ambiant astrology could develop into a real modern science, in the sense that meteorology and sociology and economics are sciences. All such sciences deal with the cycles of activity of large groups and their laws include a large coefficient of uncertainty. We must realize however that in these sciences the connections between causes and effects are relatively easy to trace and understand. The present difficulty in ambiant astrology is that *so far* we do not have anything like a clear picture of the nature of the forces at work in the vast spaces of the cosmic field we call the solar system. Yet scientists have dealt with electricity and studied the law of its distribution when the nature of electricity was unknown.

The main difficulty in transforming the events-orientated astrology into a modern science is that in the usual astrological charts we are dealing with many variables— at least ten planets, cusps of houses, nodes, etc.—and, moreover, that several frames of reference can be used and are being used: longitude, latitude, right ascension, tropical and sidereal zodiacs, etc. The type of statistics which have been used recently are quite confusing. The most painstaking and extensive ones made in France by the scientist Gauquelin at best indicate that certain positions of planets like Mars, Saturn, Jupiter, Venus are found more often than the law of chance would assume in the birth charts of related types of professional men, i.e., military men, priests, statesmen, artists. But these positions (near the mid-heaven in the ninth house, and near the Ascendant in the twelfth house) do not fit very well in the usual scheme of interpretation accepted by astrologers today. They do not refer to the zodiacal positions of the planets, a factor predominant in astrological interpretation. Above all, the deviations from the norm are too small to serve as a thoroughly reliable guide in the selection of a profession, or the selection by a large firm of a person who has to be especially qualified for a specific job. It seems evident that altogether new procedures have to be used if the effectual influence of the state of the whole solar system at birth is to be defined with a reliability of the order expected in modern sciences.

In this new ambiant astrology the welfare of individual persons as individuals would not be considered. People would be classified according to their predominant birth type with reference to the contribution they might be expected to make to humanity. Electronic brains would organize all birth data all over the globe, and people born with exactly the same charts would be watched, so that the effect of *the very same* astrological influences on say 100 persons in different social environments and with different genetic backgrounds could be compared. Marriages could be arranged on the basis of astrological affinity, etc. We would then have a situation not unlike that existing in old India under the control of the Brahmin class, i.e., in a ritualistically planned society whose structural order was believed to be constantly adjusted to the order of the seasons and of the universe. The purpose of adjustment in the future might be very different from that prevailing in the land ruled by the Laws of Manu. But if the men of the next centuries are able to ascertain the exact nature of the ever-changing relationship between human beings on earth and the energy field acting at every moment upon our planet, it should be possible to define accurately the reactions of these human beings to the energies of the solar system, reactions manifesting as precise events, scientifically ascertainable according to statistical values. A particular individual might not react as expected; he would belong to the 10 or 20 per cent of cases which do not fit—and perhaps would be regarded with suspicion as a deviate!

Such a picture of an astrological future may not seem very agreeable to many people, but it would fall in line with the collectivistic trend of our society. In the meantime, the other type of astrology, geared to the needs and the welfare of individuals, could and should gain greater respectability in official circles *provided* commercial interests would cease to cater to an uncritical public and that a basic type of educational drive were possible that would broadcast what is involved in this astrology for the individual person. It would, above all, be necessary that a sufficient number of astrologers should be willing and able to "rethink" astrology and to refuse to satisfy the demand for the forecasting of precise events. An astrology which seeks to guide individuals on the conscious way to personality integration and to a richer sense of interpersonal relationship may, of course, in many instances foresee the probability of certain *types* of events, but it is interested in them primarily as outer manifestations of turning points and phases of readjustment, or of moments of fulfillment, in the life process considered as a whole. The event *in itself* is not essential; only the phase of the process to which it points and which it will exteriorize.

Unfortunately as the collective cultural and religious frames of reference of the past traditions vanish into disturbing but no longer guiding ghostly presences, individuals feel ever more insecure. They are left to face increasingly complex decisions and choices on the basis of ego likes and dislikes; but the world of egos is a confused, hectic, and most insecure jungle. A science based on statistics cannot give us security and faith, for why should anyone not belong to the, say, 20 per cent of cases to which the statistical law does not apply?

To say this is not to deny the value of statistics in terms of large groups and for certain practical purposes, but it should be clear that such a statistical approach cannot give confidence and security to the troubled and uncertain individuals of our society in crisis of transformation.

What is needed is a feeling that each individual life is ordered and structured, yet that within this structure of destiny anything can happen and there is freedom and the great play of interpersonal relationship. *Because* there is structure and stability actual events really matter little. Each of us is a whole with a powerful rhythm undertoning all our actions. If we can come to sense this "fundamental nature" and to be grounded in "destiny" we are at the same time stabilized in selfhood.

The process of our individual existence flows rhythmically, and we—as conscious egos—can flow with it, watching the turns and the crises as they come, accepting them in the name of our total being. In this acceptance there is peace and strength—and this astrology of which I am speaking can help us, if properly used and understood, to reach such a state of consciousness.

THE STRANGE DESTINY OF LEE HARVEY OSWALD

George Bishop

The execution of Lee Harvey Oswald by Jack Ruby must rank as the outstanding single retributive act of the present century. Ruby tried Oswald, found him guilty, and executed him in full view of millions of people. In one brief pull of the trigger, Ruby bridged thousands of civilizing years and reverted to the simple, tribal relationship of prehistoric man.

According to the laws of the United States of America, Jack Ruby committed a murder not sanctioned by the state and is in dreadful violation of those laws. The case, while cut-and-dried legally, has deep philosophical implications and points up the seldom-discussed fact that individuals, when acting as executioners, sometimes perform a service every bit as morally responsible—and quite often, more so—than the most judicious, state-endorsed execution.

Certain clearly definable factors must be present for any private killing to qualify as a morally responsible act, and the circumstances surrounding Oswald's death contained them all. He committed a crime against society that aroused even the most stolid citizens to a high emotional pitch. For the first time in this century, a cry for vengeance was heard throughout the land. The need for a Jack Ruby became manifestly apparent.

The Warren Commission report settled the burden of Oswald's guilt beyond any rational doubt. He was guilty of premeditated murder, a crime that calls for the death penalty in any capital punishment state. Jack Ruby carried out that sentence.

The logical question: "What would happen if everyone took a gun and killed everyone whom they thought deserving of it?" can be answered just as logically. *Everyone* did not take up a firearm and execute the murderer; only Jack Ruby did that. Why cannot the society that spawned a Lee Harvey Oswald produce his executioner as well? The shooting of President Kennedy was no ordinary crime, both because he was President and because he symbolized the apolitical personalities of one hundred and eighty million people. Lee Oswald had *society* in the cross hairs of the Mannlicher-Carcano 6.5–mm. rifle that killed the President; and society, in the person of Ruby, brought him to justice.

Our laws are designed to deal with illegal acts that presuppose some degree of rationality. As soon as we are faced with a palpably irrational act—the act of a mentally disturbed person—we place the perpetrator of that act outside the laws that govern the rest of us and he is scheduled for special treatment. We do not say: "If A kills B and A is sane, he is electrocuted; but if A commits the same crime and is found to be insane, he is put to death more humanely by lethal gas injection." The fictional, insane A's are placed completely outside of the law and enjoy a privileged position.

What sane society, one might ask, would have it any other way? The answer must be that no just society is capable, by its very nature, of enforcing its own standards on those whom it deems to be mentally and, in some instances, emotionally below those standards. The mark of a civilized society rests in the recognition of an obligation to those less equipped, mentally and physically, to cope with their problems.

By the same token, then, must we not accept the existence of a Jack Ruby as being equally outside our society and equally removed from its laws? An irrational act left the great majority of American people powerless to react on the same plane; one of their number did react, and Lee Oswald died.

Jack Ruby, by all public accounts, is a somewhat unsavory type. The owner of strip joints and the confidante of known criminals is not the kind of man that the average American would ask home to dinner but, for that very reason, he makes an excellent candidate for an unofficial executioner. There is sound precedent for the more stable, upright members of society hiring an untouchable to do their dirty work.

If Oswald had been killed by an Ivy League graduate, a respectable father and family man who was a success in his chosen profession, *then* society might have been justified in taking a long look at itself, because the executioner would have represented the ultimate refinements of our concepts of law and order.

Jack Ruby's shooting of Lee Harvey Oswald was noteworthy for both the enormity of the original crime and the public nature of the execution itself. Not since the days of Madame Guillotine, when the people massed by the thousands in the public squares to witness the death of the individuals they considered to be detrimental to their society, has a large group of the people, this time numbering in the millions, watched the execution of a public menace.

Personal executions are nothing new, as the homicide detectives of any large city police force will be the first to concede. A man, judging his wife an adulteress, kills her. A woman, seeing her children subjected to the wanton cruelty of a resentful husband, murders him, both to protect her own and as a method of retribution. A son or daughter rebels and kills a parent. How many times has the perpetrator of this act of personal vengeance been quoted as having said: "He (or she) deserved to die?"

Private executions, no less than public, are the result of a judgment rendered following the commission of some crime, real or imagined. The relative morality of the two types of justice must be left to another discussion, what we are concerned with here are the facts of their existence and, in so far as it is possible to ascertain, the reasons behind those facts.

It takes little effort to accept a public court finding a person guilty of some capital crime, then of the state executioner carrying out the death sentence. We have directed these people to kill this man or woman in our behalf because we demand an eye for an eye, or because we hope that Sam Jones, down the street, will get the message and not take a shot at us for pinching his wife's bottom. The latter reason, prevention of future crime, is the more popular rationalization usually cited in any argument between those who support and those who would abolish, capital punishment. It is not considered civilized to admit the raw revenge motivation that guided the destiny of Jack Ruby and, vicariously, of many hundreds of thousands who mentally squeezed the trigger with him in the comfort of their living rooms.

Private execution motivations, because they usually do not directly involve us, are more difficult to comprehend. Everyone understood why Ruby shot Oswald, but not everyone understands why Mrs. Smith, after fifty years of marriage, does Mr. Smith in with a poker and takes off for Las Vegas.

Private execution, as opposed to ordinary homicide, may be defined as an act perpetrated as the result of a prior act of physical or emotional violence that constituted a threat of mortal proportions to the member or members of the immediate social group.

What fundamental difference is there between a woman shooting her husband for having forcible intercourse with his own daughter, and Caryl Chessman dying in the gas chamber for raping and robbing a number of women? The difference is only one of degree, not of kind. In fact, a good argument might be made that the woman was more justified than was the state, in carrying out an execution as a result of the respective crimes.

Anglo-American society has put a heavy premium on its individual members not functioning outside the laws of the state. In France, for example, the so-called *crime passionel,* which is nothing more than an execution carried out very much within the limits of our definition, is often handled sympathetically by the courts. Unfortunately, because the sensational press has seen fit to play up the cases involving a "woman wronged" who caught her husband cavorting with his private secretary and put a bullet in him, the great number of more mundane personal executions that have resulted in outright acquittal, have been overlooked. In Italy, too, the idea of personal justice is more realistically received.

A case may be made that the increasing, worldwide movement toward the abolition of Capital Punishment (thirty three nations and nine of our United States have now outlawed the death penalty) is fostering a resurgence of the Jack Ruby approach to the solution of personal problems. If Ruby could have been sure that Oswald would "Get what was coming to him," it might have altered the course of history.

But Ruby was not at all certain that Oswald would be punished, that is, executed, for his crime. In retrospect there is every reason to believe that the assassin would not have received what Ruby believed to be the only just sentence: death. A history of his own muddled thinking, pictures released showing him holding the assassination rifle and wearing a holstered pistol, his private bullying of his wife, and his supposed sexual inadequacies, all marked Lee Oswald as, at very best, an unbalanced individual and, at worst, from Ruby's point of view, legally insane at the time of the shooting.

Clearly, Oswald might escape state execution, therefore, according to Ruby, it remained for him to make certain that justice triumphed. Certainly both men were unbalanced. It would be difficult to deny one and accept the other, but the fact remains that the death-penalty abolitionists, although sure of their motives and steadfast in their ideals, sow doubt in the minds of the large number of nameless "little people" to whom the idea of justice remains the taking of the traditional eye.

The pros and cons of capital punishment aside (although those who advocate its abolition present the life-term prisoner a golden opportunity to rid himself of his inhibitions by the systematic murder of everyone in the prison whom he dislikes), the purpose here is to show by example that the stopping of state-sponsored executions will not alter some of man's more deeply ingrained characteristics, such as the desire for revenge and the need to make one of his own kind a symbol whose destruction results from the need of continuous guilt transference.

It would seem an inescapable conclusion that the manifestly "civilized" character of state executions is, together with the increasing trend toward abolishment of the death penalty, leading us full circle back to the prehistoric times where each man acted in his own best interests in the absence of codified laws.

Historically, man has always threatened himself with the most terrible punishment of which he can conceive, his own death, as a deterrent to doing himself violence. Cave man X said to cave man Y in effect: Come snorting around my cave and I'll bash your head in. Cave man Y, getting the message, became a law-abiding cave dweller. This same basic tableau repeated itself through history with the various complications of a developing society failing to alter the simple logic of the initial premise.

Cave man X then formed a mutual pact with Y against newcomer Z so that if either one was molested, death to Z became certain. They elected Z to represent them when A and B appeared on the scene and his safety became their safety. They wrote down what they would do to A and B if Z was molested and laws were substituted for direct threats. And so into the twentieth century, when Jack Ruby awoke the morning after President Kennedy's assassination and realized that neither he nor the late President's assassin were covered by the head-bashing restraint. He did what a frightened, disturbed man is apt to do, he lashed out, and Lee Oswald died.

The Kennedy assassination and the Oswald execution provide a classic example of the difference between the two life-taking operations. An assassin strikes against the established social order; an executioner defends it. The unassailable proof of this is that, at last gasp, the executioner kills the assassin, never the other way round.

American political history is replete with private executions that make the Jack Ruby case look legitimate by comparison. Beginning with the execution of John Wilkes Booth, President Lincoln's assassin, by his pursuers when he attempted to flee a burning barn, and continuing through the execution of Huey Long's assassin by his bodyguards (Long, shot once but very much alive, watched his bodyguards kill and then empty their guns into his assailant's body before being taken to the hospital where he later died), the public record of private executions (no one was even arrested in either case), presents the latest affair involving Jack Ruby in a slightly different light.

If one of the secret service men had shot Oswald ten seconds after the assassination he would have emerged a hero, although his act would have been as much an "illegal" execution as was Ruby's. More so, because the secret service officer is a trained gunfighter, conditioned to cool response under fire, and therefore less liable to act impulsively. His protection of the President became nugatory, as did the protection of Lincoln and Long, as soon as the assassin succeeded. There is little doubt, however, that a medal would have been struck and pinned on the chest of the agent who had brought Oswald down.

The dividing borderline between legal and illegal homicide is narrow and shifting. The relationship between state-endorsed and private inspired execution is not as rigidly defined as we might wish to believe.

One man's murder is another man's justice.

THE SOLAR SYSTEM IS INHABITED

Joseph F. Goodavage

In her will leaving a $20,000 prize in care of the French Academy of Sciences for the first Earthman who communicates with other worlds, Mrs. Marc Guzman, who died fifty-six years ago, specifically *excluded* Mars . . . so certain was she that Mars is inhabited by intelligent beings.

The announcement of this will, made in the *International Telecommunications Union Journal,* was enthusiastically greeted by five hundred delegates to a space radio-communications conference in Geneva, Switzerland.

When it comes to the question of life on Mars, almost everyone is an expert. There are nearly as many opinions as those who have opinions.

The overwhelming mass of solidly-scientific eye-witness evidence however, is on the positive side—most of it from the ranks of professional and amateur astronomers, but some from other disciplines.

Research chemist Wells Alan Webb of Berkeley, California, claims the canals of Mars are so like a man-made rail network and so *unlike* ordinary geological cracks, they indicate that something intelligent created them . . . ergo, Mars is or was inhabited.

Another chemist, who believes otherwise, boasts the support of an astronomer. Dr. Sebastian Karrer's theory is that Mars' great clouds of toxic smog automatically eliminate our last hope of finding a life-supporting planet in this solar system. He says the clouds of Mars are mostly gases of compounds of oxygen and nitrogen, "the same eye-burning, choking toxic gases of terrestrial smog." Dr. Karrer's theory received the support of Carl C. Kiess, astronomer at Georgetown College Observatory.

One of these scientists pointed out that our own fresh air might be "toxic and eye-burning" to inhabitants of other worlds, that these "toxic gases" may therefore be just plain fresh air to the inhabitants of Mars. Humans and animals breathe air, he pointed out, while fish breathe water; it is conceivable therefore, that Martians could breathe toxic (to us) gases and extract oxygen from it the way fish do from water.

All critics of the Life on Other Worlds idea seem to have been suddenly and summarily crushed by the massive, overwhelming weight of evidence that the solar system is actually a seething cauldron of purposeful activity . . . that interplanetary voyages and probably commerce have been going on for centuries . . . *scores* of centuries!

Our National Aeronautics and Space Administration (NASA), the Soviet Academy of Sciences, and a large number of world-renowned astronomers and astrophysicists are not merely satisfied that Mars is an inhabited planet; they're convinced that city-size space platforms have been orbiting our celestial neighbor for several thousands of years!

This being so, it must necessarily follow that the Martians have a slight lead on us in the "race for space." We may be a backwater world by extraterrestrial standards, but the United States has no intention of taking second place, if possible. (See *The Search for Extraterrestrial Life,* by NASA—20¢ from the U.S. Government Printing Office, Washington 25, D.C.)

Those artificial Martian satellites are the two "moons" of Mars, Phobos and Diemos, about which a strange and fascinating mystery has clung since they were "discovered" by American astronomer Asaph Hall in 1877. Nearly a century and a quarter previously, they were described in uncanny detail by author Jonathan (*Gulliver's Travels*) Swift in his *Travels into Several Remote Nations of the World* (London, 1726).

How could Swift have known that Phobos was five miles in diameter and Diemos ten? How could he have anticipated the exact names Hall would give them a century later? How could he have guessed at something so utterly fantastic in those days—that the orbital periods of the satellites were measured in *hours,* not months or years (Diemos, 7 hrs., 39 mins.; Phobos, 30 hours, 18 mins.)?

Diemos revolves around Mars in less than one-third the time it takes for Mars to rotate once on its axis. This, according to the known laws of astrophysics, is impossible. Yet Swift anticipated these astronomical facts. The question is, *how?*

His information, according to the best scholarly estimates, was derived from several extremely ancient astrological tomes which are probably no longer in existence; the original facts were probably standard knowledge among astronomers thousands of years ago.

There are only two ways in which this could have been possible: 1. Biblical and pre-Biblical astrologers had telescopes. 2. The theory expounded in Emmanuel Velikovsky's *Worlds in Collision* is correct—that Mars swung into a remarkable perigee (closest approach to Earth) twenty-seven centuries ago and was close enough for the two "Steeds of Mars" to be seen either with the naked eye or with rudimentary telescopes (Aztec pictographs found by archeologists with ephemerides, or tables of calculated planetary positions, showed an Aztec astrologer looking through a long, tubular instrument at the stars and planets. The time: B.C.).

Unpalatable as these explanations may be to the conventional minded, there seems to be no other explanation for the fact that ancient Hebrew, Egyptian, Babylonian, and Indian astrologers could have known Mars had two moons, not to mention their sizes, orbital velocities, and distances from the parent body, as was indicated by Jonathan Swift.

"Certain astrologers," he wrote in his fictional narrative in 1724, "have discovered two lesser stars or satellites, which revolve about Mars, whereof the innermost is distant from the center of the primary planet exactly three of its diameters, and the outermost five; the former revolves in the space of ten hours . . ."

Velikovsky states that Homer and Virgil were aware of the existence of the two trabants of Mars, and that their knowledge was derived from ancient astrological texts. But if Newton, Halley, Herschel, or Leverrier (who had powerful telescopes) did not discover these "Steeds of Mars," what instruments could ancient astrologers have possessed to enable them to see two tiny objects at such a great distance?

Even if Mars approached as close to the Earth as Velikovsky believes it did during its last great perigee passage (causing untold devastation to the Earth), its moons would *still* have been too distant to see without telescopes. The mystery remains. What optical instruments did the ancient astrologers possess in those days?

By some odd coincidence Asaph Hall gave the Martian moons the identical names by which they were known to the ancients: Phobos (*terror*) and Diemos (*rout*). What reason could these ancient people have had for giving the Martian moons these names—unless they were associated with the very things for which they were named?

An object five miles in diameter would have to approach much closer than our Moon to be visible to the unaided eye from Earth. If this actually happened, then Mars would have been *many* times closer to the Earth than the Moon is today.

According to the law of Roche's Limit, this is 2.44 times the radius of the planet. Mars, therefore, could have approached well within 10,000 miles of the Earth *without* being destroyed by the great magnetic-gravitational stress of such a close approach (the diameter of Mars is 4,213 miles, its radius 2,106½ miles; 2.44 times the radius of Mars is about 9,500 miles, and about double that for the Earth).

That great catastrophes actually did rend the lands and seas of the earth is reported in the writings of all ancient peoples.

Sennacherib's astrologers warned him to hasten his battle and finish off the enemy before the catastrophe struck. He ignored his advisors and was finished off himself. Isaias, the Hebrew astrologer and Biblical chronicler, who also foresaw the great natural disaster coming in the year of the Martian perigee, advised King Hezekiah to muster his strength against Sennacherib at the same time.

This close passage of Mars was recorded by all civilized peoples of these ancient times. All claim that Mars destroyed most of the world. *"The heaven he makes dark, he moves the Earth off its hinges,"* wrote the ancient Indians. *"Nergal (Mars) causes the Earth to shudder,"* said the Babylonians. *"His body fills the heavens with the color of blood,"* wrote the ancient Peruvians. Mars *must* have come quite close to the Earth in those days—close enough perhaps for living men to have seen the "moons" of Mars.

If so—and if these moons are *not* natural satellites, then the beings of Mars must have constructed and placed them in orbit more than 2700 years ago!

Fred S. Singer, a prominent American astronomer, agrees with Dr. Fred Hoyle—who is possibly the world's leading astrophysicist—that the Mars' satellites are artificial. They also find themselves in agreement with Russian planetary physicist I. S. Shklovsky who states that Phobos and Diemos are far too small to be natural satellites like our own Moon.

On January 23, 1963, NASA's Chief of Applied Mathematics, Raymond E. Wilson, said, "Space probes are now being prepared to determine if Phobos is actually a huge orbiting space base." NASA is siphoning off sixty million dollars for this project alone.

In 1959 Dr. Shklovsky, the Soviets' most erudite planetary physicist, told the Soviet Academy of Sciences that Phobos was actually an artificial satellite, probably made of aluminum or magnesium.

"We have to assume that Phobos is hollow inside," he

said, ". . . something like a tin can from which the contents have been removed. It is an artificial satellite of Mars."

Shklovsky said his evidence is based upon four peculiar properties of Phobos:

(a) No other planet has natural satellites as small as those of Mars.

(b) Phobos is only 5,000 miles from the surface of Mars; Diemos is also much too close.

(c) Phobos orbits the Red Planet at three times the speed of Mars' rotation. This is something no natural satellite is known to do. A natural satellite cannot move faster than the planet around which it orbits because both the planet and its satellites "were originally made from the same materials, traveling at the same speed."

(d) Phobos, like all Russian and American space capsules, is slowing down and falling toward Mars.

From these data, Dr. H. M. Sinton, an astronomer at Yerkes Observatory in Wisconsin, told the National Academy of Sciences, "Phobos may be a huge orbiting city filled with men, women, and children. The other moon, Diemos, might be one, too."

As one of the NASA Mars Probe scientists, Dr. Fred S. Singer, Professor of Astronomy at the University of Maryland said: "If Shklovsky's figures are accurate, then Phobos could be artificial, hollow, and therefore made by living creatures."

Astrophysicist Dr. Fred Hoyle of Mt. Wilson, Cambridge, and Mt. Palomar agrees. "This is the only theory I have heard that covers the mystery of these two moons," he declared.

Other scientists, other opinions. "Putting up such a satellite would strain the abilities of a world rich in natural resources," said one critic. ". . . the extreme poverty of mineral resources on Mars would have deprived the Martians of the necessary materials." This was Dr. Clyde W. Tombaugh's statement; he is Associate Professor of Earth Sciences at the Research Center of New Mexico University. Dr. Tombaugh admittedly has never been to Mars, so he isn't exactly certain what its natural resources might be. His opinion is based on an analysis of the Mars spectrum as light from the planet passes through a prism.

"That," retorted Dr. Singer in response to Tombaugh's statement, "is like saying the Egyptians couldn't have built the pyramids." Singer means of course, that the satellites are *there,* and that they're *artificial*—so what's the argument?

Dr. E. C. Slipher, director emeritus of the Lowell Observatory at Flagstaff, Arizona, racked up another negation of the theme. "It would be physically impossible to orbit such a huge satellite," said Dr. Slipher.

ITEM: NASA developed plans some years ago for putting huge platforms into space—platforms that will dwarf the largest ocean liners in the world. They will be sent into orbit piece-by-prefabricated-piece.

Dr. Slipher, it would seem, has been shot down in flames.

Let's assume the facts warrant a conclusion that the "moons" of Mars are space stations. Why were these satellites, particularly Phobos, orbited by the Martians?

"Their purpose naturally would be to sweep up the radiation belts around Mars to enable Martians to operate in space without radiation hazards," says Dr. Singer.

Another possibility is that they're something like life boats into which a carefully controlled population can escape during times of violent natural cataclysms on the surface.

We won't have the answers to these intriguing mysteries until our astronauts reach Mars and send emissaries to its space "cities," Phobos and Diemos. Chances are, however, that we'll encounter extraterrestrial life closer to home base long before we land on Mars.

Ever since the earliest days of Biblical times, strange sightings have been seen in the skies of Earth by a superstitious and astounded mankind. Our own "dead" Moon has been giving every sort of evidence imaginable that it is indeed inhabited by beings possessing a highly advanced technology, perhaps an alien race closely resembling humans.

Or . . . perhaps not.

For several centuries now, reputable astronomers the world over have been reporting strange objects and mysterious activity in every sector of the solar system. None other than that superastronomer, Sir William Herschel, who discovered and catalogued 800 double stars and 2,500 nebulae, said he had observed lights inside the lunar crater Aristarchus in 1783.

Conforming to what later developed into an invariable pattern, the experts quietly exchanged knowing glances and refused to look at the evidence. Nevertheless, they promptly damned all such reports into a limbo of oblivion.

But the reports of extraterrestrial goings-on refused to stay damned; in fact they increased. A Russian astronomer reported in 1958 that he had observed lights on the Moon.

In October, 1963, lights were seen in Aristarchus again. Astronomer James C. Greenacre of Lowell Observatory in Flagstaff was mapping the Moon for the Air Force. He too saw the lights and summoned witnesses to confirm the sighting. Greenacre and his witnesses saw them again in November 1963; they were in Aristarchus.

On the nights of June 4 and 5, 1964, the lights appeared once more when Greenacre was at the telescope. Unfortunately, he did not record a sighting because the Moon wasn't visible from Arizona when the lights were on.

An amateur astronomical group from Riverdale, Long Island, N.Y., however, saw a red spot on the Moon. They were using a comparatively small eight-inch telescope.

Gilbert Schmidling, leader of the group, shared his place at the eyepiece with his twenty-two-year-old son David, Glenn St. Clair, and Henry Cooper. As they took turns observing and drawing what they saw on a lunar map, a pale reddish-orange spot formed on a ridge near Aristarchus. It became a bright red glow before vanishing at 5:10 A.M.

The Moon watchers' sketches were identical.

These and similar sightings have been made hundreds of times since the turn of the century—and *thousands* of times before then. "It's fashionable to pooh-pooh a new idea," said sixty-three-year-old Schmidling. "That's always true in the earlier stages of any given science. These spots will be seen often now that they've become 'respectable.'"

Here again there are as many theories as there are sightings of the lunar lights, most of them conventional, mundane, or "ho-hum." For some odd reason, the experts have historically rejected the most obvious and logical explanation for any and all otherwise unexplainable UFO's. "Balloons," they say. Or, "Venus." Either explanation, coming from an Authority, is usually sufficient to convince the layman he hasn't actually seen what he has seen. Other conventional explanations are: "snow-flakes, birds, airplanes, seeds, spots before the eyes, insects, and mass hysteria."

This curious reaction seems most prevalent among those who haven't seen or experienced anything at all, but who nevertheless insist on telling hundreds of thousands of eyewitnesses that they haven't seen what the observers know they've seen. Many laymen are hoodwinked, browbeaten, ridiculed, or brainwashed into disbelief of their own senses, or persuaded to keep silent altogether.

Times are changing, however.

A reliable source in Washington, D.C., has it that the U.S. Air Force and other government agencies are working on large public relations programs to prepare Americans for psychological acceptance of the fact that nearby space is inhabited by several species of intelligent aliens.

Near the turn of the century, on October 28, 1899, at 4:50 P.M., M. A. Garrie saw a round luminous object rising above the horizon . . . about the size of the Moon. He watched it for fifteen minutes as it moved away, diminishing to a mere speck.

On August 7, 1900, two men in a field under an "apparently clear sky" were struck dead by lightning. Several hours later a man was killed on the summit of Mt. San Gorgionio, near the Mohave desert "by lightning." There was no storm; in fact the Sun was shining. Two days later, beneath another clear sky, a fourth man was

121

killed on the summit of Mt. Whitney . . . again "by lightning."

On May 1, 1908, between 8 and 9 P.M., a correspondent for *Cosmos* magazine reported seeing "an object, with a nebulosity and a diameter equal to the Moon's. At nine o'clock a black band appeared on the object and moved obliquely across it, then disappeared." This sighting was made repeatedly by scores of others both before and after May 1, 1908.

". . . Venus, under extraordinary meteorological conditions," said the experts. (See *The Book of the Damned* by Charles Fort)

Charles Fort, a newspaperman who gathered the most remarkable series of such "coincidences" in literary history, gives no explanation other than the fact that eclipses of the Moon coincide with the highest frequencies of sightings of lights on the Moon.

In 1845, Sir John Herschel, son of the superastronomer Sir William, saw in his telescope, "many objects of considerable size in the air, seemingly not far away." Herschel is quoted as stating the objects were masses of hay, "not less than a yard or two in diameter."

Nothing less than a cyclone or whirlwind could have sustained these masses, according to astronomer Herschel, yet the air all around him was calm. "No doubt wind could have prevailed at the spot but there was no roaring noise." None of the masses fell within his observation or knowledge.

One hundred twenty-three years later, the stuff came down in lofts at the same place.

"Dartford, England, Aug. 29 (1963) (AP)—Straw

fell for an hour over this part of Kent today, baffling one and all.

Residents soon were busy with brooms and pitchforks removing it from streets and lawns. Then the phenomenon stopped as suddenly as it had begun.

" 'We are baffled,' said the police. 'There was far too much of it for it to have been dropped from an airplane.' "

Decades—even centuries ago—bits of manufactured metal have fallen from the featureless skies. Practically all were of an unknown metallurgy. Some were said to bear engravings originating from no known language on this planet. Fort says they were "damned."

The British Isles had its fair share of oddities in recent years. One of them is a "thing" reported by United Press International to have landed in Charlton, England.

"British Army experts planned to search Roy Blanchard's potato field today for possible clues to identify 'the thing' buried under a part of it.

"Mr. Blanchard remained convinced 'some craft from outer space' landed in his field. But Leonard Carter, secretary of the British Interplanetary Society, said:

" 'Outer space ships are absolute nonsense. This crater and the markings, if they were indeed found, indicates a shower of meteorites hit the area.'

"The mysterious crater appeared ten days ago. It is saucer-shaped, eight feet wide, and has four trenches radiating out from the rim. Each trench is four feet long. In the center of the crater is a small hole.

"Army bomb disposal experts dug in the area yesterday. Later a spokesman reported:

" 'Something has been detected. But we're absolutely clueless as to what it is.'

"Mr. Blanchard has reported that all the barley and potatoes in the field disappeared 'as if they were sucked out.' He also claimed that a cow nearby suddenly began shedding its skin as though it had been scorched."

Authorities later insisted the thing "had proved to be" a meteorite. One meteorite large enough to dig a "saucer-shaped" hole eight feet wide would only be the size of your fist, therefore easily recoverable without any army bomb-disposal experts or all the other hoop-de-doo.

Charles Fort pointed out that conventionalists in science are prone to invent obvious preposterousnesses and connect them to unexplained natural evidence. In the case of the Charlton potato patch, a follow-up Associated Press release stated: "Dr. Robert Randall, who said he was an astrophysicist from Australia, figured the hole was made by a forced landing of a 600-ton flying saucer carrying about fifty men, probably from the planet Uranus."

Some astrophysicist. That was preposterous and confusing enough to suit the purpose. The thing was forgotten. If there's an astrophysicist named Robert Randall in Australia or even somebody masquerading as such, we'd like to hear from him. Maybe he was one of the fifty survivors of the crash.

More mysteries. On January 27, 1912, a Dr. Harris looked at the Moon and saw "an intensely black object." Astronomer Harris estimated its size at 250 miles long and 50 miles wide. "The object resembled a crow poised, as near as anything." Clouds then obscured vision and Dr. Harris, in a masterpiece of understatement, announced: "I cannot but think that a very interesting and curious phenomenon happened."

The crow-like object, or something like it, has been observed from time to time flying around in space near the Sun, crossing the Sun's disc—on and around the Moon, eclipsing Venus, Mars, Jupiter, Saturn, and the fixed stars.

"A dark round object passed rather slowly across the Moon in a horizontal direction," on July 31, 1896, said W. R. Brooks, director of the Smith observatory. Somebody scoffed . . . said it was a bird. The scoffer hadn't seen it. Dr. Brooks replied that it had no wings.

Then a Dutch astronomer, name of Muller, reported that on April 4, 1892, he too had seen the same phenomenon. Others confirmed the sighting. Apparent diameter of the object: about one thirtieth that of the lunar disc; the dark round object crossed the Moon's surface in three to four seconds.

An amateur astronomer was gazing at the Moon through a two-inch achromatic, power 44, at one o'clock on the morning of June 27, 1896 "when a long black object sailed past, from west to east, the transit occupying three or four seconds." He thought it was a bird, but its short, stubby wings displayed no fluttering motion.

In the early days of radio, both Marconi and Tesla reported many strange radio signals which occurred at the same times as a series of unexplained light patterns on the Moon. (Landing lights for space ships?)

During October, 1958, the tracking devices at the then Cape Canaveral Missile Center in Florida began picking up strong radio signals. Scientists tracked the object and recorded its signals, then suddenly realized they could neither identify the source nor interpret the signals. Within an hour, two giant radio telescopes in America and several more overseas were plotting the apparent position of the device from which the strange signals were coming. They easily determined the distance, position, and course of the celestial transmitter.

The signals came from something that was heading in the general direction of the Moon at more than 9,000 miles an hour. Unlike anything put into space by either Russian or American scientists, this thing changed speed and course several times.

The recordings were replayed to trace the origin of the device from which the signals emanated. It was first picked up about 3,000 miles out from the Earth, headed on a course which would have taken it to or near the Moon. The signals were recorded for three-hour periods. They stopped on contact with the Moon.

No visual observations were reported at the time.

In 1956 Ohio State University and several other observatories picked up a code-like, intelligently modulated radio chatter emanating from the planet Venus.

But the single human experience with things extraterrestrial that seems to dwarf all others occurred on a warm September evening in 1952 near Flatwoods, West Virginia. This one made the front pages of practically every newspaper in the world.

Against the nearby mountains a round object was seen by five children and a dog at play. They gazed at the thing which resembled no plane or airship they had ever seen—either in life or in the pages of any book.

It spurted streams of fire and sparks and wobbled in the air as it slowly descended, then dropped out of view among the trees.

The May children, Eddie, thirteen, and Fred, twelve,

ran to tell their mother they'd seen a plane or "flying saucer" land on the foothill that rose above the town. Mrs. May, a beautician, was understandably skeptical . . . until she went outside and saw a reddish pulsating light or glow about three hundred yards away near the top of the hill.

She sent her young sons running to summon the nearest male. They got Gene Lemon, a young National Guardsman who, armed with a flashlight against the growing dusk led a party of six up the hill. The group consisted of two ten-year-olds, Tommy Hyer and Ronnie Shaver who had also seen the thing land, Neil Nunley, fourteen, Mrs. May, and her two sons.

In the best science-fiction thriller tradition, a light mist was forming as Lemon, Neil Nunley, and the dog hurried up the brush-covered hillside about fifty feet ahead of the others. A pungent, sulphurous odor assailed them and grew stronger as they came closer. Near the top of the hill where the irritating, unpleasant odor was strongest, they saw something glowing red, like a great mass of hot coals. It pulsated, they said afterward. For the moment, curiosity overcame their natural fears and the nauseous smell that permeated the area. Followed by the fretful canine, they made their way along a dilapidated fence to an old gateway for a better view of the thing, which appeared to be about six feet high and twenty-five feet in diameter.

As they stood in the gateway, undecided, Mrs. May and the youngsters finally caught up. Their attention was riveted on the strange glowing thing on the ground about seventy feet from where they stood. For the moment no one noticed something else moving among the bushes less than twenty feet to their right—not until the dog bristled and made pitiful noises in its throat. They all whirled at once to confront . . . whatever it was. Lemon swung his light among the bushes and outlined something that by all human standards was monstrously huge.

They saw a head and the shoulders of something totally alien; it was just shy of being ten feet tall. The creature was wearing a kind of helmet which projected from "a dark blue-green or greenish-gray body which reflected the flashlight beams like rubberized silk."

It was not human, needless to say. Mrs. May's screams of sheer terror cut through the evening air.

The visitor's face was full, red, and round. It possessed two eyes that, like the eyes of cats, dogs, deer, and some fish, reflected the beam of Lemon's flashlight. They couldn't make out the lower part of the creature because of the concealing brush and weeds, but everyone agreed later that it did not walk. Rather, it seemed to slide its lower extremities along the ground, perhaps due to an injury.

There was a steady, hissing sound; a powerful sickening odor pervaded the scene. Someone estimated that it might have been trying to repair something—to stem the escape of its planetary gases, possibly something "toxic, eye-burning, and choking."

Either because of the scream or the sight of the alien, the dog yelped in terror and fled, yapping out of earshot. In that micro-second, Lemon froze and dropped his flashlight. Then all seven humans hit the panic button and ran-slid-raced-tumbled down the hillside through the darkness.

They immediately phoned the sheriff at nearby Sutton,

West Virginia. But the sheriff and a deputy were then miles away checking out a report of a plane that had crashed (it turned out no plane had crashed that night).

Word of the alien spread quickly and the residents of Flatwoods gathered. Somebody thought of calling Lee Stewart, Jr., editor of the Braxton newspaper. Stewart arrived on the scene thirty-one minutes after the incident. He found the children in a state of shock. Mrs. May was hysterical.

The editor persuaded Lemon to lead another party of local men back to the hilltop. This time they were armed.

The huge pulsating red thing was gone. So was the Being From Elsewhere (*fortunately for it*). But the same alien, sulphurous odor still clung sickeningly to the spot and there in the soil where the object had stood was a deep depression.

Off to the right, where Lemon, Mrs. May, and the youngsters had seen the creature, the editor found skid marks among the bushes. Nobody could explain such peculiar markings other than in terms of the temporarily shipwrecked alien.

The whole episode was called a hoax by some, of course —mostly by those who had never been anywhere near the place nor talked with the witnesses. A "hoax" like that one would have cost Hollywood at least $100,000. The population of Flatwoods was three hundred.

There are probably many unsuspected and unknown candidates for Mrs. Marc Guzman's 100,000 franc prize ($200,000 at current exchange rates) walking around today. Neither Mrs. May nor Mr. Lemon seem likely candidates, however. Their experience was subjected to the most minute scientific and editorial scrutiny, but the West Virginians can hardly claim to have done any real "communicating" . . . perhaps understandably so.

When the first genuine, proven dialogue takes place between Homo sapiens and an intelligent being from an alien world, there's bound to be a mad rush for priority to the Guzman prize.

Space voyagers are out there skimming among the planets, possibly the stars. They travel in vessels built by races of high technical and scientific accomplishments—perhaps on bustling worlds much like advanced copies of our own. It may even be that the planet Earth—or at least the solar system—lies along one of the regular space lanes.

If even one of the dozens of landings reported has actually taken place, and this seems highly likely, then others did also. And human beings saw them.

Claims, anyone?

Shelly Lowenkopf

NATHANIEL HAWTHORNE, SPOKESMAN FOR THE DAMNED

Nathaniel Hawthorne was a man who toiled slavishly to produce a body of sketches and novels that would represent his own spiritual, if fanciful, biography. He succeeded instead in writing a biography of the devil and the forces of darkness.

His major fear was that he should remain America's most obscure man of letters and yet during his life time, two books gave him fame. Ironically enough, he wanted to publish one, *Twice-Told Tales*, anonymously, and a Boston publisher had to plead with him for the opportunity to read the manuscript of *The Scarlet Letter*.

Today, he is all but forgotten, known only to a few scholars as a man of considerable and cloudy talents, remembered by some students as a bit of an eccentric. But when he is discussed at any length, it is generally in terms of having written the Great American Novel and for belonging to the Transcendentalists, a movement he loathed and criticized.

Hawthorne could be called a man of curious nature, or of the literary turn of mind, but both these are polite euphemisms for saying he was, at best, eccentric and, more likely a crackpot.

Even though he had Edgar Allan Poe as a contemporary rival and outspoken critic, Hawthorne is very likely the only man in American letters who was so successful in writing such utterly murky and tortured accounts with unknown forces and mysterious enemies that he frightened himself.

He seems to have been so secretive that he often forgot what he was hiding, why he was hiding it, and from whom it was to be hidden. He may even have hidden things from himself, and his some-time friend, Ralph Waldo Emerson, made entries in his diary describing Hawthorne as a fascinating man, one from whom it was virtually impossible to get any information.

For over ten years, Nathaniel Hawthorne struggled in the solitude of a small room, writing and burning endless stories and wrestling with demons of his own invention. He yearned for recognition as a writer, but published his first novel anonymously, then bought up and destroyed as many copies of it as he could find.

He more than personified New England reticence, he reeked of it. And his first major book, *Twice-Told Tales,* took its title from the fact that the stories all appeared in magazines anonymously. Nevertheless, this book might not have been published at all if a friend had not guaranteed the printing costs and persuaded him to sign his name to the book.

As hard as Hawthorne struggled with his writing, he felt himself to be lazy and he derived a perverse satisfaction in giving this impression to others. John Greenleaf Whittier said that Hawthorne "never seemed to be doing anything, and yet he did not like to be disturbed at it."

There was hardly a place he ever visited that he truly enjoyed and one friend went so far as to describe him as suicidal. He painted a habitually gloomy picture of himself and doubted he would ever be able to attract women or have friends like other men.

This was how Hawthorne saw himself and, in fact, was, to a large extent. The appellation of crackpot would not have offended him in the least. He might well have embellished on it and called himself a nut, but a darling one. And into the bargain, he might have tossed some of his more famous contemporaries such as Henry David Thoreau, Margaret Fuller, and John Greenleaf Whittier.

As others saw him, he was a bit reserved and tricky, but he was also bright, talkative, and an excellent teller of humorous stories. His journals are filled with accounts of women who seemed to like him and of women for whom he was more than fond. One of his closest friends was a president of the United States, and, however withdrawn he might appear to be, the record shows him as a competent politician, one who was strongly interested in the politics of his country and in the reforms of Andrew Jackson.

While America was becoming drunk with the results of new egalitarian politics and the thriving of the Industrial Revolution, Hawthorne was trying his hand at Brook Farm, a utopian society at which he bravely attempted to farm and ranch before giving up the whole thing as a botch. All during this time, however, he was deep in thought, turning out stories which could be called science fiction. They certainly dealt with time travel, confrontations with demons, and the transformation of inanimate objects into persons. All these devices were handled with a deftness and reality that is worthy of Isaac Asimov, Clifford D. Simack, and other modern science fiction authors.

After he reached his peak of fame with *The Scarlet Letter* and followed it up a year later with *The House of the Seven Gables,* he was sought out by the literary world, which he attempted to shy away from.

Thoreau, Emerson, and Herman Melville sought his company, but he preferred less literary people as friends. Margaret Fuller, an admitted Transcendentalist and woman's rights champion, was fascinated by him, but Hawthorne was put off by her directness. He once wrote her a letter telling her that her sister and brother-in-law were most unwelcome at his home. While he was at the Transcendentalist oriented Brook Farm, trying his hand at communal living, he wrote his soon-to-be wife, ". . . the number of cows is now increased by a transcendental heifer belonging to Miss Margaret Fuller. She is very fractious, I believe, and apt to kick over the pail. Thou knowest whether in these traits of character she resembles her mistress."

The one literary figure who was most exuberant and determined to become fast friends was Herman Melville, who ultimately dedicated *Moby Dick,* his finest work, to Hawthorne. Speaking of his mentor, Melville said Hawthorne was noble, good humored, and intricate, but behind his eyes was "a blackness ten times black . . . a great power of blackness," which came from Hawthorne's "Calvinistic sense of Innate Depravity and Original Sin, from whose visitations, in some shape or other, no deeply thinking mind is always and wholly free. . . . Perhaps no writer has ever wielded this terrific thought with greater terror than this same harmless Hawthorne."

Hawthorne very possibly lived a double life, each at odds with the other, but each in its own way contributing to the output of literary work which secures the man's reputation and each adding fuel to the notion that Hawthorne is an exemplary prototype of a mystical eccentric.

Although he seemed to function quite well in it, reality was not his cup of tea, and it is difficult to assess whether his roots are in reality and his growth in a fantasy world or just the reverse. When he was not deeply involved in his dark, tortured world, he was busy making copious notes of reality, describing such things as his wildly successful marriage, some of his tedious jobs which were won through political contacts, and even detailed accounts of his children as they played on the floor and clambered over him as he sat at his writing desk. If he did lose his temper at such times, he was careful not to lose it before he got the details of his children's activity down in ink in his journal. And as such, we are left to wonder about the true function of these copious journals, which he never intended for publication. Were they to serve as anchors to reality when he cast himself into his own special worlds? Or were they to serve as food on which his deprived victims, his guilt-ridden Puritans, his conscienceless monsters and demons would feed on?

The fact is that Hawthorne's use of his own notes and journals was the least effective when transformed into his fiction. Such works as *The Blithedale Romance,* which borrowed heavily on his days spent with the Transcendentalists on Brook Farm, were among his crudest, not so much betraying his bewilderment with the world about him as his greater ability to find conflict in the past or in the darker reaches of men's consciences. But his native ability and humor were of such a high order that *The Blithedale Romance* might have been every bit as compelling and important if Hawthorne had been able to view it from a more generous perspective in time, say fifty years.

Although he had no professed religious affiliations and, indeed, rejected the prevalent Unitarianism out of hand while gradually losing respect for all clergymen, Hawthorne was still the product of Puritanism. One Hawthorne biographer, Henry Seidel Canby, says it is impossible to comprehend Hawthorne without the Puritan background. It was for him a "fortress from which he had escaped and was glad to be gone, and yet looked back to as a city fortified and strong in its certainties . . ."

Another Hawthorne biographer, Mark Van Doren, puts the matter of heritage to even sharper use: "Witchcraft for him was not fiction, it was fact; he still experienced its mystery and its guilt."

This expression of background came to its finest moment in *The Scarlet Letter,* a novel of strongly Puritan backgrounds and universal conflicts. Although Gothic in style, it is the first American tragedy and it has been called "The Puritan Faust." The action of the story commences in front of a prison and ends in a cemetery. In between, we find seduction, guilt, and fear; dark men roam the forest; and, although she is portrayed as essentially good—good but fallen—Hester Prynne, the adulteress-protagonist, is seen in the same mysterious forest. In the most sensual scene of the entire novel, Hester meets her lover and lets her luxurious black hair tumble down her shoulders. They do not touch nor do they speak. And the similarity between the Hester of this scene and a witch celebrating a Black Mass is not entirely lost.

Hawthorne said *The Scarlet Letter* was a hell-fired book. When he finished reading it aloud to his wife, there were tears in his eyes, his voice was choked with sobs. However, it is the shorter fiction which illustrates the wide range of occult subject matter Hawthorne used when he unwittingly wrote his long, diabolic biography.

His most famous short story, "The Minister's Black Veil," is the one most often used to introduce high school students to the world of symbolism and, erroneously, to Transcendentalism. In this sharply focused tale of horror, the Reverend Mr. Hooper wears a black veil over his face at all times. This veil is made particularly real and frightening by Hawthorne's description of it as it flutters with Hooper's every breath.

Perhaps its greatest effect as allegory is the immenseness which may be read into it. Indeed, it may be considered in some ways a dramatization of the author's very secretiveness. We are never told in so many words *why* the Reverend Hooper wears the black veil, but it is certainly something a country with a Puritan heritage could accept and has later become a symbol at which an age with Freudian interest could shudder.

Hawthorne said the black veil enabled Hooper "to sympathize with all dark affections." Hooper's death enabled him even more; while he is dying, he says, "I look around me and, lo! on every visage a Black Veil." This includes the parishioners, but it also includes the reader.

"Alice Doane's Appeal" is probably the earliest published story he wrote. It deals directly with Salem witchcraft, incest, fratricide, duplicity, and double identity. Contemporary morality is more realistic in "My Kinsman,

Major Molineaux," where young Robin travels from the country to Boston in order to take advantage of the connections his illustrious uncle might arrange for him in the business and professional world of the city.

From the moment of Robin's arrival in Boston and his search for the home of his uncle, there is a feeling of dread and foreboding. On two occasions, he meets a man who seems similarly to be seeking Major Molineaux, and although this man is never called by name, his saturnine appearance leaves little doubt that he is Hawthorne's devil. As the reader moves from place to place with Robin, it becomes increasingly apparent that there is something ominous brewing, and finally, it becomes evident that it is going to happen to Major Molineaux. Robin is the last to learn, but learn he does; Major Molineaux, his illustrious clansman who is to give Robin a baptism in the city life, is slated that very night to be tarred and feathered by an angry mob.

Another gloomy tale springs from Hawthorne's own journals: "The human heart to be allegorized as a cavern; at the entrance there is sunshine and flowers growing about it. You step within, but a short distance, and begin to find yourself surrounded with a terrible gloom, and monsters of divers kinds; it seems like hell itself. You are bewildered and wander long without hope."

A less haunted but nonetheless frightening approach is his tale in which a rich man wills his mansion and estate to a poor couple. "They remove into it, and find there a darksome servant, whom they are forbidden by will to turn away. He becomes a torment to them; and, in the finale, he turns out to be the former master of the estate."

These Hawthorne tales all seem attended by haunts, laments, screams, and secret agonies. Many are parables, such as "Young Goodman Brown," the story of a young man who leaves his pretty wife one evening for a stroll in the woods, that primitive New England place of terror where witches' anthems ring out regularly. Brown will soon have an encounter in the woods and in it, he will either dream or experience the discovery that evil exists in every human heart. Hawthorne remains coldly distant, allowing the reader to guess whether the experience is dream or reality. The encounter is with the Devil, who awakens in Brown the consciousness of sin; this is the sin of his ancestors who persecuted Quakers and killed Indians, the sin of the Puritans and Quaker elders who still live.

Remembering his pretty wife and the pink ribbons she wore in her hair when he left her, Brown shouts out in agony at his visions. And then there is "a scream, drowned immediately in a louder murmur of voices, fading into far-off laughter as the dark cloud swept away, leaving the clear and silent cloud above Goodman Brown. But something fluttered lightly down through the air and caught on the branch of a tree. The young man seized it and beheld a pink ribbon."

And so, Brown is shown the dream or the reality of sin in everything to which he is linked by love and heritage. Returning to Salem in the morning, he encounters his wife, overjoyed at seeing him. She dashes to meet him, her pink ribbons fluttering, and nearly kisses him in front of the entire village. Brown, still not sure if he has dreamed or not, has been irrevocably changed and the sight of his wife's ribbons becomes the ultimate horror. He has undergone a Hawthornian transformation and is doomed now to be a cynical, distrustful man who will see evil everywhere, even where it does not exist. He is rooted to the collective guilts and fears of his past and present, and his innocence is gone as surely as Adam's was gone after one bite of the apple.

"The Birthmark" is another dipping into allegory, mixing scientific probability with art and morality. H. Bruce Franklin calls this story no less than science fiction, and in it Aylmer is fortunate enough to have in Georgiana a wife with only one imperfection, a birthmark on her cheek. Being a man of science, Aylmer discovers a potion which will remove this tiny flaw, thus leaving Georgiana without "the crimson hand, which . . . had been strongly visible on the paleness of Georgiana's cheek . . ."

He induces her to take the potion, then sits back to await the results. Gradually, she sinks into a sleep and the offending birthmark begins to fade.

> "By Heaven! it is well nigh gone!" said Aylmer to himself, in almost irrepressible ecstasy. "I can scarcely trace it now. Success! success! . . ."
>
> . . . These exclamations broke Georgiana's sleep. She slowly unclosed her eyes and gazed into the mirror which her husband had arranged for that purpose. A faint smile flitted over her lips when she recognized how barely perceptible was now that crimson hand which had once blazed forth with such disastrous brilliance as to scare away all their happiness. But then her eyes sought Aylmer's face with a trouble and anxiety that he could by no means account for.
>
> "My poor Aylmer!" murmured she.
>
> "Poor? Nay, richest, happiest, most favored!" exclaimed he. "My peerless bride, it is successful. You are perfect!"
>
> "My poor Aylmer," she repeated with a more than

human tenderness, "you have aimed loftily; you have done nobly. Do not repent that, with so high and pure a feeling, you have rejected the best the earth could offer. "Aylmer, dearest Aylmer, I am dying!"

Alas! it was too true!

Aylmer has his moment with a completely perfect wife, a moment in which she takes her dying breath. Then a hoarse, chuckling laugh is heard, a laughter that is really the mockery of all the Dark Forces.

These are the stories of the man who could sustain the dark, terrible suspense and anguish of *The Scarlet Letter*, the man who could make profound suggestions for yet another dark allegory, *Moby Dick,* and the man who could hope to make enough money for his impending marriage by editing and writing the *American Magazine of Useful and Entertaining Knowledge.* This was the man who had his richest financial rewards as a result of his interest in politics and for his biography of a president of the United States, Franklin Pierce.

This was Nathaniel Hawthorne, who dipped into the occult world of the soul, the psyche, and the netherworld of man's existence to write allegories and terror tales for adults and jolly textbooks and readers for children.

Modern critics with a Freudian turn might rely heavily on Hawthorne's repressed sexuality and his Puritan heritage, but they must invariably come a cropper. In his lifetime, Hawthorne had three successful and deliriously happy marriages; one with his devoted wife, Sophia, one with the occult, and one with words. Perhaps each, in its way, pained him at times, but he did not die a sad man nor a broken man. Shy, reticent, and at ease with only a handful of intimates, Hawthorne was not a fond traveler or a demonstrative man, but he took trips to uncharted areas where very few had been before him, wrote outrageously sentimental love letters to his wife, never betrayed a friend, and kept his secrets to the last.

HENRY DAVID THOREAU, CHILD OF NATURE

Henry David Thoreau had an appearance that was as "ugly as sin, long-nosed, queer mouthed." He was "an intolerable bore . . . tedious, tiresome, and intolerable— the narrowest and most notional . . . And yet . . . he has great qualities of intellect and character."

This was the man who lived largely by himself in the wilderness and wrote about it in the simple, straightforward *Walden,* his most famous work. A graduate of Harvard at the age of twenty, he was "bred to no profession; he never married, he lived alone; he never went to church; he never voted, he refused to pay a tax to the state; he ate no flesh, he drank no wine, he never knew the use of tobacco, and, although a naturalist, he used neither gun nor trap."

The first description of Thoreau was from Hawthorne, the second from Ralph Waldo Emerson. Thus, a shy, sensitive man was seen by the most reticent and the most outgoing of his peers. To turn the tables for a moment, Thoreau was more fond of Hawthorne; he felt Emerson was patronizing him and he did not go out of his way to curry favor with this admitted poobah of the Transcendentalist movement.

If Edgar Allan Poe was the first Bohemian in America,

Thoreau was certainly the first Beatnik. He spent two years and four months at the famed Walden Pond in Massachusetts, building a shelter, cultivating land, and reading the Greek classics by oil lamp.

His journal has inspired naturalists to believe he was a great conservationist; Transcendentalists eagerly adopted him as living proof of their own manifest spiritual destiny; philosophers have taken him over bodily as an example of man's prevailing spirit of survival; modern students have made him a monarch of civil disobedience; and Freudians have claimed him as an embodiment of the id.

Thoreau could also be looked upon as a hermit, a mystic, and a man with an expanded consciousness. The fact is that he very probably was all these and, as Hawthorne has suggested, a bit of a bore. The further fact is that Thoreau put in his years at Walden Pond more out of curiosity and lack of any outward direction than from great ethical convictions. To be sure, he wanted very much to see if he could sustain himself in the wilderness within the confines of his meager wallet, but more than anything else, he was bewildered by civilization, relying on it more for the comfort of abstract ideas than any hope of sustenance.

His years at Walden and in other forests and wilds heightened his sense of nature, and his journals are a frequent revelation of his delight at visits from birds and animals. These wilderness sounds and ways were his ultimate education, so much so in fact that in the future, whether in the forest or the drawing room, Thoreau was always hearing the sound of a different drummer.

He was already a prime candidate for a mystical point of view that was very much a working tenet of Transcendentalism, that of the mystical forces found in nature.

It was these very forces to which Thoreau brought his good education and his sense of simplicity. One particular incident at Walden Pond seems to have focused his attentions on a point of view he would carry for the rest of his life.

This incident took place while Thoreau was camping with friends, two white men and an Indian. They all sat by the fire at night while the Indian sang songs in his native tongue. At length, Thoreau gave up his attempts to write down the words, settling, instead, on listening to the words and accepting them as a voice from the past, a mystical voice of the forest.

While the others slept, Thoreau pondered the quality of aloneness that always brought to him "messages" from the surrounding woods. Finally, he slept, but it was not a deep sleep and suddenly, he awoke to the sound of a loon.

Noticing that the fire had fallen apart, he got up to bunch the logs closer together. He discovered at the edge of the smouldering sticks an elliptical ring of white light, about five inches in diameter and perhaps a quarter of an inch wide. Unlike the redness of the other coals, this light glowed as a pure white. Immediately, Thoreau was taken by it. He prodded the stick with his finger and found it to be cold. With his knife, he pared away the bark and cut off chips, realizing that he had found a piece of phosphorescent wood.

I was in just the frame of mind to see something wonderful, and this was a phenomenon adequate to my circumstances and expectation, and it put me on the alert to see more like it . . . I let science slide, and rejoiced in that light as if it had been a fellow-creature. A scientific *ex-*

planation, as it is called, would have been altogether out of place there. That is for pale daylight. Science and its retorts would have put me to sleep; it was the opportunity to be ignorant that I improved. It suggested that there was something to be seen if one had eyes. It made a believer of me more than before. I believed that the woods were not tenantless, but chock-full of honest spirits as good as myself any day,—not an empty chamber, in which chemistry was left to work alone, but an inhabited house,—and for a few moments I enjoyed fellowship with them.

This fellowship was to return, again and again, in different forms, but always with the same effect. Henry David Thoreau, bright, probing, and facile of mind, was to bore his friends on occasion, inspire them on others, and confound them in general. But from this time on, it scarcely mattered to him; he had his journal and he had animals and birds, with whom he held long conversations. In fact, he probably held animals in higher esteem than people, and his journals are filled with the accounts of his attempts to communicate with them and learn from them.

Of Thoreau's friends, Van Wyck Brooks reports many who were wild:

. . . he had the breams [fresh water fish related to the carp], who nibbled from his fingers, while he stroked them gently and lifted them out of the water, the muskrat that emerged from the hole in the ice. The muskrat looked at Henry, and Henry looked at the muskrat, wondering what the muskrat thought of him,—safe, low, moderate thoughts, of course. Muskrats never got on stilts, like some of the Transcendentalists. Once he conversed with a woodchuck, three feet away, over a fence. They sat for half an hour, looking into each other's eyes, until they felt mesmeric influences at work over them both. Then Henry moved closer and spoke to the wood-chuck, in a quasi-forest lingo, a sort of sylvan baby talk. The woodchuck ceased to grit his teeth. Henry, with a little stick, lifted up his paw and examined it; then he turned the woodchuck over and studied him underneath.

Such an attitude could hardly be without repercus-sions, the best example of which is from James Russell Lowell, then editor of *The Atlantic Monthly,* who ob-jected strenuously to a paragraph of Thoreau's which intimated that pine trees might, indeed, have souls, which were possibly intended to soar into a higher heaven than the one reserved for men.

This approach may have upset, even scandalized Lowell, but it did little to change the opinions of Thoreau's contemporaries who, as Transcendentalists, were vitally concerned with man's ability to mobilize energy and thought and rise above or beyond artificial limitations.

By modern standards, Thoreau would be classified as a Beatnik and a pacifist and heard from accordingly at sit-ins, rallies for academic freedom, and Ban-the-Bomb marches.

"I have paid no poll tax for six years," he said. "I was put into jail once on this account, for one night; and, as I stood considering the walls of solid stone, two or three feet thick, the door of wood and iron a foot thick . . . I could not help being struck with the foolishness of that institution which treated me as if I were mere flesh and blood and bones, to be locked up."

This was the incident in which he was reportedly discovered in jail by Emerson, who said, "Why Henry, what are you doing in here?" And Thoreau, so firm in his cause against paying any taxes to support war and slavery, is alleged to have shown such surprise at Emerson's toleration of these evils that he said, "Why Waldo, what are you doing out *there?*"

It is probably an apocryphal story, along with the implications that Emerson paid his fine. But the arrest is entirely like Thoreau, who was strongly vocal on all civil and individual rights matters and who, at one time, took up the cudgel against railroads as being destroyers of the countryside: "We do not ride on the railroad; it rides upon us. And if railroads are not built, how shall we get to heaven in season? But if we stay at home and mind our business, who will want the railroads?"

Individuality was the very least of his problems and one of the many things which came easy for him. "I make my own time," he said. "I make my own terms. I cannot see how God or Nature can ever get the start of me." His own terms involved a naturalness and simplicity that is quite nearly occult in its implications. He was quite sure that man's happiest prospect would come from building his own home, raising his own food. Far from leaving him simple and unsophisticated, this would prepare man for a universal enjoyment of civilization, of nature, and of God. If Thoreau had any feeling of the occult, it was on this level of approach.

Because he made his own time and lived in his own way, he was not as prolific a writer as many of his contemporaries, and probably thought of himself less as an author than as a man writing to keep the records clear for humanity. From his educational background and his association with such men as Emerson and Hawthorne, it is only natural that he should have kept rather detailed journals of his impressions. In this sense, he was particularly worldly; his writings were done in the practical spirit of the Renaissance man, who wanted records of everything to further his own education and awareness of the world.

Two books during his lifetime, some personal notebooks, some poetry, and a few articles for magazines, articles on the order of "Civil Disobedience," were the total output of a man who died at age forty-four.

Although he professed no interest in spiritualism or the world of psychic phenomena as such, he is not without appeal for the occult minded. His dialogues with animals are only one aspect, his attempts at transcendental projection are yet another. A good example is his description of a dream during which he had a stimulating conversation with an acquaintance, Bronson Alcott. The moment he awakened from the dream, he thought:

> . . . I was a musical instrument from which I heard a strain die out . . . My body was the organ and channel of melody, as a flute is of the music that is breathed through it. My flesh sounded and vibrated still to the strain, and my nerves were chords of the lyre. I awoke, therefore, to an infinite regret,—to find myself, not the thoroughfare of glorious and world-stirring inspirations, but a scuttle full of dirt . . .

In diet, posture, and ability to visualize things, he is almost the perfect embodiment of the Zen spirit. He is certainly at the stage of preparedness discussed as necessary for advancement in such Eastern mystical religions as Vedanta, Hindu, Buddhism, and Zoroastrianism. More likely than not, he would have considered excursions into these worlds, had he lived longer. His journals reflect his familiarity with "the great Hindoo philosophies" and his reverence for all living things is manifest.

He went to the woods in order to live deliberately, "to front only the essential facts of life, and see if I could not learn what it had to teach, and not, when I came to die, discover that I had not lived. I did not wish to live what was not life, living is so dear; nor did I wish to practice resignation, unless it was quite necessary."

He wanted to and did live "deep and suck all the marrow out of life, to live so sturdily and Spartan-like as to put to rout all that was not life, to cut a broad swath and shave close, to drive life into a corner, and reduce it to its lowest terms."

Very probably, he tacitly accepted the probability of reincarnation because he speaks of his desire to drive life into a corner, and reduce it to its lowest terms, and, "if it proved to be mean, why then to get the whole and genuine meanness of it and publish its meanness to the world; or if it were sublime, to know it by experience, and be able to give a true account of it in my next excursion."

Thoreau was certainly prepared for living in this world. Although he did not visit such wide swaths of it as Emerson, Howells, Herman Melville, or Mark Twain; although he did not carry forth such burning messages, he was intimately acquainted with the things he did see and adequately prepared for the things which might be revealed to him.

The experiences of life were very much to him like the many experiences he had at night. "The night," he said, "is oracular. What have been the intimations of the night? I ask. How have you passed the night? Good night!"

MARK TWAIN, THE GENTLE CYNIC

Mark Twain died in style and, characteristic of the man, left works for posthumous publication which greatly resemble literary time bombs—or even better, literary firecrackers—which are still going off, much to the bedevilment and amusement of his readers.

He had been given an honorary doctor's degree at Oxford; his works were translated into foreign languages; his European lecture tours were rousing successes; his rages and ripostes against carefully chosen victims produced hearty laughter. Two of his works, *The Innocents Abroad* and *The Gilded Age*, helped forge the American character in a manner no one has since approximated.

Nearly sixty years after Twain's death, such scholars as Justin Kaplan are still found, devoting five- and six-year chunks of their lives to the writing of definitive biographies which properly assess the power and effect of Twain, his life, and his work. In the past ten years, there has scarcely been a publishing season in which some new book on the man has not been issued. This includes his San Francisco correspondence (a former source of newspaper income during his lean years), his columns in a Buffalo, N.Y., newspaper (after his popularity had been forged), his letters to his daughter, Susy, and, at the very least, new editions of older works with new introductory material added.

This is all by lengthy way of establishing Mark Twain as a prolific author with a profound influence on his own and subsequent generations, a man whose worst books were best sellers and whose best books have become classics.

From his first early essays which he signed with the pseudonym of "Josh" and sent to the no-holds-barred frontier newspaper, *The Territorial Enterprise* in rich, raucous Virginia City, Nevada, to such final works published in his lifetime as the misanthropic *The Mysterious Stranger* and the cynical *The Man Who Corrupted Hadleyburg*, Twain worked hard at his craft and relentlessly edited himself to produce a deceptively simple, pointed, and lucid prose.

But in spite of the signs which point to Twain as a highly skilled craftsman who was carefully aware of his audience, it is rather easy to raise the question: Did he really know what he was doing when he wrote his numerous books, essays, and short stories?

Did he know what he was doing or was he guided by a force he could barely explain to himself and rarely control?

It is not an easy question to answer, but one which should be raised, largely because of his interest in the paranormal, the development of the unconscious, the dependence on intuition, and the preoccupation with telepathy, for which Twain had his own description, "mental telegraphy."

The fact is that *all* these forces had some effect on Twain's work and personality, on the way he saw himself, and, of equal importance, on the way he feared others would see him.

He wrote an essay entitled "Mental Telegraphy" in his early forties, nearly at the peak of his popularity. The work was all set for inclusion in *A Tramp Abroad*, but the author removed it because "I feared that the public would treat the thing as a joke and throw it aside . . ."

The public did not throw it aside although Van Wyck Brooks, a later Twain commentator, did, passing off Twain's preoccupation with the occult as being typical of the author's boyish nature, his puckishness, his love for pranks, leg-pulls, and dead-pan jokes.

When "Mental Telegraphy" finally did appear, it was published in *Harper's Magazine* eighteen years after it had been written, causing none of the criticism Twain feared and bringing him such reactions that he included it in a new book, *The American Claimant and Other Stories and Sketches*. The subject remained an active one and he included "Mental Telegraphy Again" in yet another book, *Literary Essays*.

During this time, Twain's interest in the subject led him to apply for membership in the Society for Psychical Research, an affiliation he maintained until seven years before his death. He did not recant on his membership, nor was there any record of a rift leading to his disassociation.

At this stage of his interest, Twain was writing about the manner in which he could demonstrate "that people can have crystal-clear mental communication with each other over vast distances."

In a letter he sent to the Society for Psychical Research, accepting membership and specifying that there was no element of privacy involved in his interest, "There being nothing furtive about it or any misstatements in it," Twain all but describes the phenomena of automatic writing. He stopped short of this, but he did leave an important clue.

... mental telegraphy as I have been in the habit of calling it, has been a very strong interest with me for the past nine or ten years. I have grown so accustomed to considering that all my powerful impulses come to me from somebody else, that I often feel like a mere amanuensis when I sit down to write a letter under the coercion of a strong impulse.

Bridging the gap between his letter and fiction writing is not so tenuous as it may sound. And keeping his words "powerful impulses" in mind while considering the way Twain regarded himself, a closer look is in order.

In his lifetime, he subjected himself to many influences, particularly those of his wife, Olivia; his friend and editor, William Dean Howells; and another close friend, the Rev. Joseph Twitchell. Some commentators have built lengthy cases to show Twain deliberately subjecting himself more to the censorship than the influence of these people, making the bulk of creditable work he produced seem even more remarkable.

But this focus on Twain will belie any notions of censorship or his desire to be a social climber. It will reveal an amazing and almost inescapable influence that Twain hadn't the confidence to call by proper name; the thing he called his intuition or U.C. (for unconscious) was his own finely attuned ability. And when he gave himself up to this "influence," the results transcended mere quality and approached enduring grace. He broke nearly all the rules he had forged for the more cautious Mark Twain and was on the firmest ground. As a result of that "influence," his works now live to tell the tale.

In his personal journals, Mark Twain referred to himself as a jackleg novelist. This nineteenth century term was one which was synonymous with an impostor or incompetent workman. For Twain, it also meant a poseur, an interloper among the literary giants and Mandarins of his day. Men such as William Dean Howells, Brett Harte, Ralph Waldo Emerson, and Oliver Wendell Holmes were personages Twain admired with the same enthusiasm a youngster today might show for the likes of Mickey Mantle or Sandy Koufax.

He sincerely believed that it was only his understanding of humor and his ability at telling the humorous story that kept him in this august company he so much admired and sought. But because this humor often proved too effective, Twain believed it was not easy to control and that it was "getting him in bad" with the very people whose friendship he courted.

With humor, he was on his firmest ground and became his irrepressible best. But let's compare one disastrous result of his humor with his earlier fear for the publication of his essay on "Mental Telegraphy."

Twain had been invited to give a keynote speech at an *Atlantic Monthly* dinner commemorating the birthday of John Greenleaf Whittier. While poking fun at himself, he also poked fun at Emerson, Longfellow, and Oliver Wendell Holmes. His joke fell flat and Twain was at once busy writing letters of apology. To his editor, Howells, he wrote:

> My sense of disgrace does not abate. It grows . . . best that I retire from the public at present. It will hurt the *Atlantic* for me to appear in its pages now . . . It seems as I must have been insane when I wrote that speech.

That was not the reason for Twain thinking of himself as a jackleg; indeed, he did not write that opinion of himself for another fifteen years, but the notion was firmly planted by this time and ready to work on him.

As a result, Twain quickly realized that there were comments he would not and could not make public during his lifetime, but he stubbornly continued to refine his techniques and approaches, using humor as a cover-up and adopting a hard shell of cynicism on which he traded.

As he came to know his audiences and techniques better, his impishness got the better of him. Under the guise of humor, he began to attack excessive romanticism, academic prejudice, frilly Victorianism, and the affected niceties of the Gilded Age. Mercilessly, he pared these excesses from his own work and attacked them in others. In such articles as "Fenimore Cooper's Literary Offenses" and "How to Tell a Story," and in essay-like digressions in nearly all his novels, Twain firmly employed humor as a tool to postulate the very rules we now consider an effective approach to fiction.

Some of Twain's rules are:

A tale shall accomplish something and arrive somewhere.

The personages in a tale shall be alive, except in the case of corpses, and the reader shall be able to tell the corpses from the others.

An author shall use the right word, not its second cousin.

Employ a simple and straightforward style.

Twain, a shrewd man, knew his audience well and from experience. He knew the importance of adhering to the rules which would seem to insure most success. Yet in almost every instance, when Mark Twain sat down to write fiction, he violated nearly every rule, every approach he had forged so carefully and consciously.

He wrote about places he had not seen, about times of which his knowledge was only the most superficial, and about people of whom he knew very little, if anything. He wrote in dialects he could not possibly have heard spoken in his lifetime, and he proposed blithely naive or outrageous substitutions for existing systems which offended him.

From his pen came two booklength essays, stoutly defending two women he had never met (Joan of Arc and Harriette Shelley) and a rather famous polemic directed against Mary Baker Eddy. With some of the finest rules at his command, Twain was still given to moods or tempers that had him cast planning aside.

In spite of this tendency, there is a believability about Twain that defies comparison, and even his most preposterous suggestions contain enough sound authority to make them accepted as plausible and appropriate. A monumental example is found in *Huckleberry Finn,* where Jim, the runaway slave, seeks his freedom by riding a raft *down* the Mississippi River, deeper into slave territory, instead of seeking a more practical means of escape, via the Underground Railway into one of the neighboring free states.

Intuitiveness plays a heavy role in this aspect of Twain's rule breaking. After all, he'd been "burned" several times and needed some standard of judgment that would let him know how far he could go. After the dismal failure of the *Atlantic Monthly* dinner, Twain resolved not to be caught again. Dipping into his early schooling in humor at the hands of his newspaper friends and associates such as Joseph Goodman, Artemus Ward, and Dan De Quille, Twain resorted to the device of telling outrageous and dead-pan lies, supporting them with equally bogus information to make them seem true. He became successful in "taking in" millions of readers, but perhaps he was his own best goat.

His contemporaries did not see him as a social reformer nor as a bona fide commentator on social matters, not, at least, in a critical sense. And so Twain promptly solved this by reserving his most pungent comments for publication after his death and cloaking everything else in the veil of humor or satire and, in some cases, "children's stories."

These attitudes caused him to set great store by his own dreams and telepathy, deliberately cultivating a dependence on inspiration to provide suitable form for the material that teemed in his imagination. "Whenever there is doubt," he said, "the right way to treat the subject shall have come to you from that mill whose helpful machinery never stands idle—unconscious celebration . . . the U.C. [unconscious] will find it if you give it time; which time will not be short of two years and will often be nine. I am speaking from personal experience."

His long friendship with this process led Twain through a career involving millions of words and hundreds of successes, financial and critical. But it is with the writing of *Huckleberry Finn* and subsequent events that the intuitive and unconscious forces come home to roost with the most effect. It was an unusual set of circumstances that caused Twain to obey nearly all his carefully formulated rules and instincts and it is almost a capricious decision that forced him into a position where he "had to" obey his instincts. The result was a book of sustained power, effect, and importance. In later years, Twain achieved this same power again, but only in sporadic bursts, and never again with the strength achieved in *Huckleberry Finn*.

When he began this novel, it was Twain's notion to cash in on the earlier success of *Tom Sawyer*, a book originally intended for adults. But when advice from friends such as Howells and his wife prompted him to make *Tom Sawyer* a book slanted for younger readers, Twain felt the same set of circumstances could hold him in good stead with *Huckleberry Finn*, both financially and critically.

Naturally, he was wrong.

Although the same, precise photographic quality of *Tom Sawyer* was used in *Huckleberry Finn*, the technique took hold, intuitive forces flourished, the entire project ran away from him and the result was a masterpiece.

Briefly, here are some of the reasons:

Twain intended to make Tom Sawyer more of a dominating character, but the lure of developing Huck Finn took control. In symbol and reality, Huck Finn probably meant more to Twain than any other character he had created. There was an intuitive feel of identification with the famous bad boy of literature, an identification Twain could use almost without further thought and certainly without excuse.

Because of other projects on which he was working at the time, Twain chose the first person narrative form as his approach to *Huckleberry Finn,* a fact that "limited" him to expressing his feelings more openly.

Because of his preoccupation with such exotic locales and situations as *The Prince and the Pauper* and the science-fiction time travel approach to *A Connecticut Yankee in King Arthur's Court,* Twain deliberately limited Huck Finn to material he knew intimately, from first-hand experience.

While he simultaneously preoccupied himself with more complex moral matters in other projects, in *Huckleberry Finn,* Twain deliberately wrote of current moral issues and described current types of folk heroes who spoke in language Twain knew well and who reacted in manners he had experienced.

Other reasons reflect Twain's desire for success, his anxiety to retire from the writing of novels, and his own self-image. This was also the period in which Twain considered himself a jackleg, a preoccupation that led to an entire book on the subject by Robert Wiggins. Twain seems to have shown an extraordinary awareness in the *Huckleberry Finn* project, creating his characters and treating them and the situations involving them realistically. "But what happened to them was not consciously his affair," Dr. Wiggins says, "they acted out their story controlled only by Twain's intuitive selection of event. . . . When he contrived plot and situation in advance . . . he fell into difficulty trying to appropriate characters and force them to obey the demands of plot."

Although this methodology might not be the best way to tell a story, Wiggins concludes, "it seems to have been the most fruitful for Twain and perhaps accounts for the reason why his achievement was to remain uneven—even within his greatest work."

It also shows what we might have missed had Twain gone in for more formal education and hints at the possible results if he had given his intuition more exercise to dictate its own terms of composition.

The fact that Twain and his wife considered *The Prince and the Pauper* his finest novel may show indications that he was not the best judge of his own work, not consciously.

When he relied on his intuition, he produced works of great control and impact, and his cynical look at himself as a jackleg is for us, his readers, to deny with finality.

Twain's image of himself as a cynical troublemaker persisted, and he honestly believed it would be better for all concerned if he left certain of his works for posthumous publication. These are all works which might have profited from a fictional and intuitive process, works which might have been even greater if the author had given himself over to his amanuensis who dabbled in the occult and the unconscious.

In spite of all the tasks he set for himself, it is to the credit of his greater genius that he was able to "cut loose" on occasion, or, to use his words, "to sneak some literature."

It is not distracting to Twain or the occult when his work is viewed in this light; it is of interest that his work is so very real and so enduring. If Twain ever was a cynic, deep at heart, he was a gentle cynic, a man who cared deeply and abidingly.